T0339821

MARIE JAËLL

Marie Jaëll

The Magic Touch,
Piano Music by Mind Training

Catherine Guichard

Translated from French by
Cyrille de Souza

Algora Publishing
New York

No portion of this book (beyond what is permitted by
Sections 107 or 108 of the United States Copyright Act of 1976)
may be reproduced by any process, stored in a retrieval system,
or transmitted in any form, or by any means, without the
express written permission of the publisher.
ISBN: 0-87586-305-1 (softcover)
ISBN: 0-87586-306-x (hardcover)
ISBN: 0-87586-307-8 (ebook)

Library of Congress Cataloging-in-Publication Data

Guichard, Catherine.
    Marie Jaëll : The Magic Touch, Piano Music by Mind Training /
Catherine Guichard.
        p. cm.
    Includes bibliographical references and index.
    ISBN 0-87586-305-1 (soft : alk. paper) — ISBN 0-87586-306-X
(hard : alk. paper) — ISBN 0-87586-307-8 (e)
    1. Jaëll, Marie, 1846-1925. 2. Pianists—France—Biography. 3. Pi-
ano—Instruction and study. I. Title.

    ML417.J342G85 2004
    786.2'092—dc22

                        2004010297

Front Cover: Marie Jaëll, courtesy of Bibliothèque National et Uni-
versitaire de Strasbourg

Printed in the United States

ACKNOWLEDGEMENTS

My thanks are due first of all to Ms. Ethèry Djakéli, a Georgian concert pianist. She studied with Eduardo del Pueyo, professor at the Royal Conservatory of Bruxelles, who, in turn, had studied with a student of Marie Jaëll. Piano teaching is a labor of love between teacher and student, and its mysteries are handed down directly across generations. Ms. Ethèry Djakéli rekindled my wonder for piano music and initiated me into the mysteries of Marie Jaëll's pedagogy.

My thanks are due also to Ms. Thérèse Klippfel, the sole legatee of Marie Jaëll's non-published works. She has donated all of them to the University of Strasbourg so that musicians and researchers can have access to them. She has authorized me to use them freely.

I also thank the Association Marie Jaëll, and its center for the training of piano teachers, from which I graduated and where I now teach.

I am grateful to all who have helped me in the preparation of this book, from technical advice to assistance with the translation, especially Sheila and David Llewellyn; Prof. B. Jaulin, Professor at the Ecole des Etudes en Sciences Sociales; Prof. Ezzat Bakhoum, Professor of Physics at the New Jersey Institute of Technology; and Cyrille de Souza who helped put my "poetic" French into "orderly" English and who assisted me with research on musicology, piano acoustics and history and kept me abreast of new findings on topics related to music as reported in *Nature, Science, The Economist* and *The New York Review of Books*.

This is not an academic book. My professional competence is strictly limited to piano pedagogy. I have freely drawn on the work of distinguished scholars of musicology, history, neuroscience, philosophy and aesthetics. The traces of their ideas and phrases are strewn throughout my book. A list of authors whose ideas went into its making will be found after the epilogue. Here, I must mention three whose work helped me formulate my argument. at About the time I was starting to write, Charles Rosen's "On Playing the Piano" appeared in *The New York Review of Books* and discussed issues dealt with here. Anthony Hopkins' *Understanding Music* explained the dynamics of European music. Finally, *Five Lectures on the Acoustics of the Piano*, edited by Anders Askenfelt, were of invaluable help in attaining a deeper understanding of Marie Jaëll's pedagogy.

TABLE OF CONTENTS

PREFACE

This book is an outgrowth of my work as a piano teacher for over twenty years. For my lessons, I follow the pedagogy pioneered by Marie Jaëll. Her insights, ever since I discovered them as a student, have been a source of inspiration for my teaching. They implanted in me her passion for the piano. I try now to instill that passion into my students. Hopefully, this book captures that passion and brings to life a deeply spiritual and lovable personality.

Probably referring to the violin, Shakespeare asks, "How is it that cat guts can hail the souls from men's bodies?" In the same vein one wonders how a piano can set anyone on fire. As musical instruments go, it is gigantic and its cast-iron frame houses a concentrated tension of over twenty tonnes.[1] Yet it pours forth crystalline sounds that move man in his inmost being.

But the piano has a double parentage. It was born of musicians' drive to exploit harmony in order to express personal emotions; and it is also a prized product of the Industrial Revolution. Thus, it is a paradox that a "monster of modern technology" should hold the key to "a purely spiritual universe, a system of ideally moving forces."[2]

---

1. "Piano," *Encyclopédie de la Musique*. (3 volumes) Edition Fasquelle, Paris 1958; and on CD, ALSYD Multimedia, 2003.

1

Marie Jaëll grappled with that mystery throughout her life, and she came to the conclusion that the true instrument of music is not the piano, but the pianist, himself. Her guide in her life-long endeavor was Franz Liszt, the arch-Romantic, and his shadow loomed large in her life.

This book weaves together three themes: the cultural life of nineteenth century Europe, the Romantic vision of music that finds its fullest expression in piano sounds, and Marie Jaëll's creativity in piano pedagogy. Her work revolved on the three dimensions of music: harmony that is vertical, rhythm that is horizontal, and the infinite that is reached by fusing the first two to conflate space and time. To her, all art, and piano music in particular, should be a gleam of the divine that sets aglow man's inner essence.

"A deeper understanding of the sound generation in the piano now seems less remote."[3] But a century ago Marie Jaëll intuited two components of a piano sound: "prompt sound" or "thump sound," contributed by the vibrations of the instrument as a machine, and "after sound" or "singing sound," produced by the strings; the first, a footprint of the Industrial Revolution, the second, a symbol of the Romantic Revolution. This essential distinction underpinned her touch technique.

"Artists are, in a sense, neurologists who unknowingly study the brain with techniques unique to them."[4] This unusual view sums up Marie Jaëll's approach to piano teaching. She unearthed deep links among tactile, visual and aural sensations in piano playing. Her discovery led her to found a piano pedagogy, called "the touch," based on the creation of "right body images" of fingerings in the brain. She convincingly argued that "the dissociated finger movements become artistic only if their image pre-exists in the brain."[5] She believed that the pianist's entire being must first vibrate with the intentionality of the music he is going to play on his piano.

---

2. Schenker H., *Harmony*, The MIT Press, Cambridge, 1954, p.xxv.

3. Askenfelt, *Five Lectures on the Acoustics of the Piano*, p.1

4. Zeki, S., Artistic Creation and the Brain, *Science.*

"It is something of a scandal that contemporary discussions in philosophy and psychology have so little of interest to tell us about consciousness."[6] In contrast, Marie Jaëll put consciousness at the core of her pedagogy, first by highlighting the intentionality that underlies all music, and secondly, by insisting that only what is consciously acquired can be transmitted. She led the battle against all piano teaching that was obsessed with mechanical and thoughtless skills. She believed that the brain images of fingerings must have a content that is first consciously understood and internalized.

As a Romantic, Marie Jaëll lived the mysterious bond between emotion and music. Naturally, emotion held a central place in her piano pedagogy. Unfortunately, "emotion has been ignored in music research until recently because it is very hard to study."[7] Indeed, "it is a source of sadness that one can search the pages of most harmony text-books in vain for any mention of emotional effect that is the magical and mysterious element in music."[8] Wonder overtakes us as piano sounds waft us to an inner universe where the clutter of industrial machines cannot follow us. Yet, the "mystery remains why melody, harmony and rhythm are so important to us,"[9] though they have no obvious biological or survival value to the humans.

"With the rise of harmony, a piece of music becomes a symbolic re-creation of the relationship that exists in a single musical sound among the consonances of its harmonics."[10] According to Marie Jaëll, such a web of harmonic relations, driven by goal-oriented movements with forward surges and continuous returns, is the core of melody and rhythm. The harmony-centered

5. Jaëll, M. *Les Rythmes du Regard et la Dissociation des Doigts*, Association M. Jaëll, Paris, 1998, p.1

6.Searle J., *Minds, Brains and Science*, Harvard University Press, 1984, p.16.

7. Benzon W., *Beethoven Anvil :Music in Mind and Culture*, Basic Books, 2001.

8.Hopkins, A., *Understanding Music*, p.32

9. *Nature*, March 7, 2002, pp.12-14.

10.Schenker.

piano music truly brings into being a musical paradise that recalls "the heaven of the great Buddhist God *Indra*, consisting of an infinite net of pearl strings where in each pearl all the others are reflected, and in each reflection the infinite number of pearls is seen again."[11] Marie Jaëll was convinced that her touch method was the pathway that would lead a pianist to that paradise by guiding him to master the increasing delicacy of sensations of his entire being and to refine indefinitely the thought that governs the musical movement.

Marie Jaëll viewed music as a goal-oriented movement. She analyzed tactile, visual and aural sensations involved in piano play in neural terms where a millisecond is a long time. She came to the conclusion that the pianist's brain refines rhythms down to their infinitesimal level and then synthesizes them following the idea embedded in them. The consciousness that is at the core of her pedagogy is the outcome of "such micro-consciousnesses."

Marie Jaëll was above all a born pianist. She embraced science to uncover the links that join music, emotion and the touch. She believed that a true pianist lives "an altered state of being" as he creates a "soundscape" suffused with the intellectual, sensual and emotional intentions of music. This book is written by a lover of piano music to share Marie Jaëll's passion for the piano with other lovers of piano music.

11. Mumford, D., et al., *Indra's Pearls: The Vision of Felix Klein*, Cambridge University Press

INTRODUCTION

This work presents a portrait of Marie Jaëll, a French musician of exceptional destiny, in the form of a voyage. She was a piano prodigy, composer, and revolutionary pedagogue whose career unfolded at the turn of the nineteenth century. The portrait will be drawn in little strokes and touches. We first give it form, features and movement; then we add color; and finally we impress on it an overall harmony by investing it with meaning and charging it with emotion. To discover the multiple facets of her personality, we search out her roots and her homeland, and meet the people who knew, loved and influenced her. We also draw on the heritage she has bequeathed to us in her writings and musical pieces. Our one objective is to disclose the passion that consumed her life.

Marie Jaëll lived in an epoch in full upheaval, an epoch of sweeping economic and social changes. The waning decades of the nineteenth century were bristling with revolutionary ideas but still anchored by the roots of tradition. Rich in vibrant Romanticism, especially in literature and poetry, the century was in quest of new forms of expression. Painting broke loose from old conventions and embraced an impressionist style. Artists probed and broadened their techniques, and the new paintings were a wonder. Music

5

seemed to limp behind other arts. Then, suddenly, harmony took bold steps, and French music in particular took off, innovating in timbres, rhythms and audacious harmonic combinations.

We are still in full Romanticism. The twentieth century is not far off, and ideas travel, jostle and prompt innovation and research in artistic as well as scientific domains. Exploration of the unconscious takes its first steps. Modern psychology, which will change man's view of himself and will have a decisive impact on pedagogy, becomes a science.

A child of her times, Marie Jaëll, born in 1846, was a true Romantic at heart, not only as an artist and composer but as a pioneer and even as a scientist in her research on musical aesthetics. Her life encapsulates all the noblest tendencies of a dynamic and creative epoch.

The first stopover on our voyage will be Steinseltz, a village in northern Alsace. Marie Trautmann was born there. Her homeland, with its rich history, was a victim of its geography — torn between two powerful neighbors. Imbued with its culture, Marie cherished the beauty of its landscapes and the poetry of its changing skies and meandering waterways, and treasured the cultural influence of France and Germany.

Political life was stormy as the century was nearing its end. The Franco-Prussian War (1870) was a watershed, wrenching Alsace from France. Marie Jaëll, deeply attached to her country, experienced the French defeat as a personal drama. Her correspondence bears witness (at length!) to her distress. In 1918, she welcomed the return of Alsace to France with boundless enthusiasm: "Flags flutter at the windows, the bells are ringing.... My happiness permeates all the forces of my being, and I feel I am fully alive."[12]

Our voyage, as we sketch this portrait, takes us to meet the people among whom she made her life and with whom she forged

---

12. Jaëll, M., Letter to a friend.

deep friendships. In the first place comes Alfred Jaëll, an illustrious pianist from Trieste, a virtuoso acclaimed all over Europe. Marie married him in 1866, joining her life to his; and he launched her into the music world of that era. Together they moved about Europe, giving concert after concert. He knew all the great masters personally — Brahms, Liszt, and Rubinstein. All of them paid handsome tributes to Marie's musical talents.

Brahms, who became one of her best friends, wrote in 1888: "How insipid are these young pianists who play the same pieces by Liszt! But speak to me of La Jaëll! A truly intelligent and spiritual person."

Indeed, Franz Liszt was foremost among her friends. A genius as composer and interpreter of music, he played a decisive role in shaping her destiny. One day he confided to the critic Albert Soubiès, "I am keen to introduce you to Marie Jaëll. She is unique; she has a philosopher's brain and an artist's fingers." On the following day the critic went to the Conservatory of Budapest and found Liszt and Marie Jaëll playing four hands. He then understood the luminous precision of the great master's judgment. A close friendship united Franz and Marie, two artists passionately attached to art and music. Inspired by him, she would deepen her reflections on musical art. By closely observing his performances, she would orient her research to musical aesthetics and pedagogy. Her theoretical work was to be indissolubly intertwined with his playing.

Another distinguished musician who was close to Marie was Camille Saint Saëns, her teacher, admirer and later a friend. He would say of her, "Marie's first attempts have been tumultuous and excessive. They looked like the eruption of a devastating torrent. But, since then, calm has fallen on her gentle nature; every day she perfects herself in her art; she does not lose sight of her objective for a second; she will succeed."

When she became the first pianist in the world to interpret the complete works of Liszt, Saint Saëns declared: "There is only one person who knows how to play Liszt; it is Marie Jaëll."

From among Marie's admirers, let us quote Catherine Pozzi, writer and poet, and a member of the *"Tout Paris"* circle at the turn of the last century. Her meeting with Marie Jaëll marked a milestone in her life. Several pages of her diary, published in 1987, speak eloquently of it. "No human figure is as fascinating as Marie Jaëll," she writes. "I think the sentiment that radiates from her is grandeur."[13]

Paul Valéry observed that Marie Jaëll was endowed with an enquiring and deep mind. He added that the writings of Madame Jaëll never left him indifferent.

Surprisingly Marie, a professional musician, learnt to be quite at home in a totally different domain, especially during the second half of her life. Her work on piano pedagogy attracted the personalities of the scientific world. Charles Féré, an eminent physiologist, sought her out and proposed to collaborate with her in research on the knowledge of hand and physiology. He lent her his scientific authority and backed her studies by his methods of systematic experimentation. After her husband's death, when Marie devoted herself entirely to research on the *"Art of the Touch"* so that everyone might realize beauty through the piano, she found in Charles Féré the unfailing support of a friend and the precious collaboration of a researcher intensely interested in the study of the hand, touch and human intelligence.

Many other persons gravitated around her. Most of their names are familiar and evocative. But what remains of Marie Jaëll, now? What do we know of her?

It is said that, "a person is really dead when the last person who knew him is dead." Since there is no longer anyone who can recall a living image of Marie Jaëll, we turn to her works; we explore her books that form an immense and varied corpus. They are, in turn, scientific, political, philosophical and even mystical. They are alive and intense, for they record her inner awareness in an age of turmoil.

---

13. Catherine Pozzi's Journal, Ramsay, Paris, p.69

They bear the stamp of an extraordinary personality. Above all, they embody her tremendous passion for the beauty of piano music.

There are also other writings, like her texts for piano teaching, her copious correspondence, and her musical pieces. Most of them are now published. Finally, there is her diary, running into hundreds of pages sculpted by her thick and stressed writing. From her work and the testimony of her friends, colleagues and pupils, what picture can we draw of this musician who embraced science to probe her art?

A portrait reveals what we want to see in it. It always flaunts meaning as a lure to hold the viewer under its spell, so we are free to stop at its features and forms. We may also wish to go beyond them and envision the mystery they hide. We are free to be moved or unmoved by the look that illuminates it. The most important thing is that it moves because we are moved.

Who, then, was Marie Jaëll?

An artist, certainly, wholly dedicated to the service of her art: a many-sided artist, a genius interpreter, an original composer, a revolutionary pedagogue, but much more. She was a creative mind who searched for the links that unite man to the mysteries of art. In her diary we find her wondering, "Why do philosophical ideas pursue me everywhere? They are reflected in all that I do. I cannot be just an artist. My art seems to me only an eternal symbol of the infinite into which we gaze our blind looks."[14] In all her work she sought clarity of thought, musical meaning, coherence and logic.

The different stages of her life saw her plunge headlong into several domains, which her restless mind was eager to study, and relate them to her art that was music. Hence the riches buried in her immense work, the result of a long life of labor, reflection, and encounter with the great minds of her time.

If we are asked to sum up Marie Jaëll's life and work in one word, we will choose "passion."

---

14. Jaëll, Marie, Journal (unpublished)

"It is not love, it is not frenzy that I have for my art... It is passion that overcomes all obstacles."[15] She has such a passion for her art that she had an overwhelming desire to understand it, and nothing would stop her flaming heart from reaching her goal. What she feels instinctively, and with a lively intuition, she seeks to disclose to the world. She is determined: "I must go beyond the stage of instinct and arrive at knowledge."[16] Her ambition and desire drive her to find ways to liberate the awareness of the interpreter, to make him be conscious of the links between cause and effect, between musical thought and tactile sensitiveness, between the brain and the hand. For, according to her, "it is impossible to perfect anything that lies in the unconscious."[17]

As a result of her in-depth research on the ties that bind the pianist to his piano, Marie Jaëll invented a method for piano teaching, and named it "Touch." It is based on a profound knowledge of physiology and tactile sensitiveness.

To know how to express and discover the musical language of a piece means to know what holds together the sounds of a group, to know how to feel and prepare the pianist's hand to express the language of the sounds. But this awareness of the sensory links that join the pianist to his instrument finds a deeper echo in us: a total awareness of what we are and of what we could be. Here Marie Jaëll broaches the complex problem of human nature and ventures beyond the boundaries set by human psychology, for musical perception and its psychic impact belong to two distinct worlds, one measurable, the other indefinable.

She notes in her diary,

> It is within us that are found our riches, our possibilities and our limitations. We must direct our eyes on ourselves, know ourselves; we must not fear to bring into the open what we are.

---

15. *Ibidem*
16. *Ibidem*
17. *Ibidem*

We never descend low enough to see what we are, we do not ascend high enough to see what we ought to be... If we want to live we must know ourselves...Like the phoenix that is reborn from its own ashes and flies to the highest summits, we can soar, we can surpass ourselves, if, after having known our imperfections, we resolve to reduce them to ashes.

In 1894, Henri Bergson forecast that the exploration of the unconscious in the substratum of the spirit with specially appropriate methods would be the main task of the new century. And such was the task that Marie Jaëll pursued: to release our resources, to bring them from the shadows into the open, and to place them at the service of musical expression. The unconscious she probed was not the *dada* of Freudian psychiatry but the part of the mind where we store the images of the world since the "ascent of man."

Her passion to come to grips with her art drove her to another passion: science. Science became her ally, and the study of geometry, physics, and physiology helped her unravel the hidden laws of aesthetics to the musician and distil a judicious blend of different sciences to underpin her method of touch.

She always claimed that technique and art are indissolubly linked. But a mere understanding, a mere knowledge of a work of art does not fathom its mystery. At most, it can determine it with precision and fix the limits where it begins. In order to be touched by a work of art we need to isolate, lay bare, and separate from all confusion its transcendent pure quality that enshrines liberty and beauty, for it is in our inner silence that we perceive its glow and depth; and then, we accept the gift of emotion.

"My mind subjugates my bodily forces which all become echoes, echoes of an ideal beauty. Such a measure seems like a liberation of our being, which not only aspires to beauty but which can attain it in its supreme fullness."[18]

18.*Ibidem*

Such a sublimation of relations between man and art, between the interpreter and the expression of musical language, begins with the perception man has of his body, and even quite simply, of his hand.

To be aware of the hand is to perceive movement or immobility, to feel the fingers that are part of it as independent elements, to develop its tactile sensitiveness to which we do not pay much attention. A hand, a hand that is made sensitive, conscious, and maintained open and immobile in space, vibrates at the contact of this space and becomes aware of its relation with it.

The infectious enthusiasm with which Marie Jaëll undertook the exploration of uncharted domains lets us glimpse her full philosophy of life.

This young woman from a peasant family in Alsace was drawn by an irresistible vocation towards art, and enjoyed her success. What, then, is the inspiration that led her, after enjoying the triumphs of her profession, to withdraw from the world, to lead a lonely and almost obscure life, and devote herself entirely to the research that became her passion?

A letter addressed in 1913 to her pupil and friend Catherine Pozzi betrays her secret. "As a child, I read Shakespeare, Homer, Dante with great respect as if I understood them. I was left with one highly particular impression: on seeing in an engraving the mystical rose which Dante held in his hand, I said to myself; if I were in his place I would hold the rose upside down to look at its roots." This comment on the image which she cherished as a child reveals her boundless passion for research and illustrates the drive that inspires all her work: Be not content to admire the flower, but study the root that gave it life and made it grow and blossom.

Marie Jaëll would pursue her research till her death in 1925.

1. Marie Jaëll and Her Century

Her Heart Had Wings

Winter 1865 –1866.

One evening Jeanne comes home all excited, throws down her music rolls, and slumps into the nearby armchair. Lise, her mother, asks her, "What's up? You seem full of excitement!"[19] "What's up? It's unbelievable: Marie Trautmann is going to marry Alfred Jaëll. They will be a famous couple."

Taken aback, Lise drops her book. "Miss Trautmann is marrying Alfred Jaëll? But he is twice her age!" Jeanne shakes her head, "No, he is only fifteen years older than she."

Lise silently meditates on the news. Marie Trautmann, the prodigy pianist from Alsace, is joining her destiny to Jaëll's, another virtuoso whom the European capitals fight over. She lifts her head, "Are you sure? How do you know?" Jeanne starts to giggle, "The gossip in the music class. For once, it must be true — our teacher told us."

---

19. Jeanne, Lise and Schuré were friends of the Trautmann family.

Lise is lost in her thoughts. Marie Trautmann ... Yes, often cited as a model. A girl, touched by God's hand, giving concerts all over Europe for years, already, with dazzling success...

"So, Marie is dreaming of raising a family. She's nineteen, a normal age. What about her career, then?" Lise turns her thoughts on Marie's fiancé from Trieste, who strides through the world of music as a conqueror.

Alfred Jaëll's reputation was already made. This traveling virtuoso was a remarkable interpreter of music. The critics always extolled his playing, delicate and full of softness. He captivated his public by the wealth of his sounds, and above all, by his marvelous trills. At the time, he was often represented with ten-fingered hands. His trills were the admiration of Liszt, who acknowledged his inability to reproduce them. Rapt audiences would listen to him play for hours, without showing the least impatience. His concerts were eagerly awaited, and the halls were always packed to the gills.

His prestige and renown led to his appointment in 1856 as the pianist at the court of King of Hanover. He played for princes and royal highnesses. The *Journal of Salzburg* reports:

> Alfred Jaëll, the pianist of the royal court of Hanover, had the honor of playing a certain number of Chopin's pieces and some of his own compositions in the apartment of Her Majesty Empress Caroline Augusta and before the following personalities: His Imperial Highness Charles Ferdinand and Arch-Duchess Sophie, Her Majesty the Queen Marie of Saxe, Her Imperial Highness the Arch-Duchess Clementine, Princess de Salerno and Mme the Duchess d'Aumalo.

Born in Trieste into a family of musicians, Alfred Jaëll took to the keyboard early. He gave his first concerts at the age of six. Then followed travels in France, Italy and Belgium. In 1843, his parents settled down in Vienna so that he could work with Czerny, the highly respected teacher of Sigismond Thalberg and Liszt. His concert tours brought him triumphs in Holland, Italy and Belgium. During a visit to Stuttgart at the age of thirteen he met Liszt, who introduced him to the Court of Wurtenburg. He then wanted to play in Paris, the center *par excellence* of musical and artistic life in those days and a magnet to all artists. In 1846, Alfred realized his dream, and left for the cultural capital, where artists immediately took notice of him.

Chopin's decision to take him as a pupil was a consecration for a lad of fifteen. Jaëll worked with the great pianist throughout the winter of 1846.

His reputation as a virtuoso was such that Barnum, the famous American impresario, spotted him and offered him a contract. Thus, at the age of twenty, Alfred Jaëll set out on a piano concert tour of the United States of America. His first performance in New York, on November 15, 1851, was an unprecedented success. Then followed tours to all the big cities of North America: Montréal, Toronto, Boston, Philadelphia, and elsewhere. He returned to France in 1854, wholly exhausted by the 400 concerts he had given during his stay overseas. The critics were full of praise for him and his technique: "A striking originality singles out Mr. Jaëll. This virtuoso does not belong to any school and his playing does not smack of any imitation."[20]

In 1864, his concert reviews were glowing:

> At a concert, listen to Liszt, or Thalberg or Rubinstein or Alfred Jaëll; each of them has his own individual and characteristic sound, a well trained ear will not fail to notice. Make the piano sing, obtain from it the roundness and duration of the sound, cover all the nuances of expression from alpha to omega, from fortissimo to pianissimo, subdue and render the keyboard sensitive by a wonderful delicacy of touch, reproduce, by I do not know what secret faculty, all the timbres of the instrument ... That is what Alfred Jaëll accomplishes with undeniable perfection. That is what makes him one of the masters of the modern keyboard.[21]

---

20. *Revue et Gazette Musicale*, May 1860, BNUS, Fonds Jaëll Mn Jaëll 37
21. BNUS, Fonds Jaëll, mn Jaëll 35

He could be called a true artist, since he knew how to render palpable the historical sentiment or the archaic color of a work. He had a pleasant character. He was a jovial little person, full of enthusiasm, with his face lit by sparkling eyes. He was popular and had many friends, especially Brahms and Liszt, whose concert pieces he often interpreted. He contributed greatly to spreading their music across Europe, and he was not shy to interpret their latest, sometimes unpublished, works.

A dedication by Liszt's hand on the handwritten manuscript of "The First Concerto for Piano," which Alfred played in public even before it was printed, bears witness to the close friendship between the two musicians: "To Alfred Jaëll, in friendly testimony of his courage to make known infamous compositions like this Concerto, from his affectionately devoted F Liszt, Weimar, April 30, 1857."[22]

Alfred Jaëll first met Marie Trautmann in 1866 in Germany. They probably ran into each other at one of his concerts. There was indeed a fifteen-year age gap between the great virtuoso and the young pianist; and he fell in love with her. The rumor of a union between the two musicians spread fast.

Jeanne was right: they became a famous couple.

In 1866, Marie Trautmann had turned twenty. Her future seemed to be traced out in a promising direction. From the beginning of her music career, she was recognized as an accomplished pianist. She was totally immersed in her art. She was scarcely thinking of marriage. Encouraged by her mother, she accepted Alfred's proposal. The wedding was fixed for the month of August, and the engagement was celebrated in Paris. Liszt was present, but hardly suspected the extraordinary destiny of the young woman he was meeting and the important place he would take in her professional life.

Though she was still very young, her talents at the piano were well known. Also, her independent and warm-hearted character

22. BNUS Fonds Jaëll, mn Jaëll 56.2

was taking shape. Since her very early age she had given concerts in all the major cities of Europe. Her triumphs were different from those of Alfred. The critics were unanimous in declaring, "her playing surprises, rather than charms!" The public and the critics were impressed not only by her sure and precise technique, but by something more that seemed to overflow from her nature, "touched by God's finger."

An assessment that appeared after a concert in Nuremberg describes the impression left by Marie when she played:

> When Marie Trautmann is at the piano her entire being is transfigured. She vibrates with enthusiasm for her art. She forgets all her surroundings. She plays only because she is driven by an inner force.
>
> Unconsciously, we are tempted to compare her to Clara Schumann, the last great artist we have heard. We do so, less to establish similarities than to single out what distinguishes these two great artists of equal value. The style, so expressive and so full of soul, of Clara Schumann wafts us on to a soft dream. We admire her deep understanding of the great masters. She interprets them with unparalleled love and accuracy. She knows how to give the least *Lied* its relief.
>
> In contrast, Marie Trautmann sweeps us over and stirs us up. When she takes over her instrument we feel we are in the presence of a creative genius, who, without betraying the composer, knows how to breathe her personal temperament into the sound matter. Sustained by a technique of the highest order, she overwhelms all our being and transports us to higher spheres."[23]

While she was still young, critics detected in her, in addition to her special talents, a nature that was filled with passion. An article in the *Bamberger Zeitung* devoted these few lines to her when she was around ten, "All the qualities are fused together in this rich talent so as to make of her a unique apparition in the history of the piano."

---

23. Kiener, p. 26.

She never aimed at producing any effect. She drew her art from the inmost depths of her soul.

Marie Trautmann managed to avoid the pitfalls that often await precocious talents. At the crossroads where so many child prodigies get lost and disappear without leaving a trace, she had the luck and courage to eschew all traps. She surmounted dangers by her natural candor as an artist and by her conviction that she was serving the noble cause of art and beauty.

Marie came from Steinseltz, a village between Strasbourg and Wissembourg, in Alsace, where the countryside is beautiful but rugged. She was raised in a peasant family, steeped in tradition, even if it was relatively well off. Her father was the mayor of the village.

Music seemed to have taken possession of her from her very first years. The peals of the village church bells enchanted her, and she would listen to them in veneration. She enjoyed the music of gypsies who trekked through her country with their violins and songs, so much so that she wanted to follow them. She was deeply in love with nature, and contemplated trees at length. In delight she would listen to the chirps of birds and the murmurs of waterways.

At six, Marie heard a piano for the first time. Fascinated by its sounds, she wanted a piano for herself. She gave her parents no peace. Her stubborn insistence was such that they soon yielded to her wish. She took to piano music with such fervor that no one or nothing could stop her. She braved the severe cold, frequent in northern Alsace, to go to her piano lessons, and her progress was phenomenal. Soon she was giving her first concerts. By the age of nine, Marie, the young peasant girl with complexion turned dusky by the sun and air of the fields, had become a pianist of note.

"The most interesting piano concert of the season," reported a journal of the time, "certainly was the one given by Marie Trautmann." The critics of the most important journals were unanimous in recognizing her talents. Her teacher Moscheles forecast that "This child will do something great in the domain of art." The prediction was soon fulfilled. The warm applause lavished on her by Rossini lent credibility to that prophecy. "This child plays the most difficult pieces of Mozart, Beethoven, Mendelssohn and Herz not only with extraordinary technique and perfect execution but also with rare understanding, deep musical sentiment and purest refinement."[24]

In December 1856, Mme Trautmann took her daughter to meet Henri Herz. After listening to Marie play, he immediately took her under his wing, and she perfected her art with him. In the meanwhile, accompanied by her devoted mother, she continued her concert tours. She even went to London in 1857 and played before Queen Victoria who, charmed, gave the child pianist a jewel as a gift.

In 1862, she enrolled at the Conservatory of Paris. After four months of study there, she entered a competition and won the first prize. On this occasion her teacher Herz offered her a magnificent grand piano that would later accompany her on her concert tours.

"On seeing Mlle Trautmann's ease and self-assurance in dealing with all the difficulties," a critic said, "one would never guess that she has just finished the Conservatory."[25]

Most artists would be content to finish at the level where she began.

The wedding was celebrated on August 9, 1866. Then the couple began an intense and rich musical life in Europe, which was in full expansion.

The newlyweds set up home in Paris at 43 rue St Lazare. Their apartment very quickly became a well-known salon. They gave concerts that soon became famous and were attended by men of letters and musicians.

One morning early 1867, Jeanne, who had come to Paris to perfect her own piano playing, received a sealed letter from her friend Edouard Schuré, the philosopher and writer. "My very dear friend, are you free tomorrow evening? Say yes, and I will take you to

---

24. Kiener, p. 23.

25. Kiener, p. 25.

a private concert, which alone is worth all the others of the season. You will hear two genius musicians; I do not say two pianists, which they are, I say two musicians! You will go back home in ecstasy. Yours, Ed. Schuré."

Edouard Schuré? Jeanne was surprised. He, so reserved in general, after all had found artists whom he admired! Intrigued, she accepted the invitation. The following evening Jeanne asked her friend (who had come to fetch her in a two-door sedan), "But, where are we going? Among what unknown people are you taking me?"

Schuré smiled, "Unknown people? People too well known, my dear; all of Europe is talking about them!" Jeanne, puzzled, looked at the address at which the sedan had stopped: 43 rue Saint-Lazare.

A staircase led them to a door. They rang the bell, and entered a spacious salon where they heard several voices whispering. Jeanne noticed a large room, an elegant audience, and two grand pianos facing each other: two big, beautiful, wide open pianos.

Jeanne was increasingly puzzled. Then she saw a young woman stepping forward to greet her; she introduced herself as Marie Jaëll.

Marie Jaëll? Jeanne was stunned. Marie Trautmann, spoken of so highly for such a long time, and now married to Alfred Jaëll, was before her, smiled to her, and then moved away to rejoin the group.

Schuré then sat Jeanne down next to him, and the concert began a little later.

For the rest of her life she would treasure the intense emotion she felt that evening. Did such a splendor really exist? Marie's playing seemed to touch the soul, and outstrip the frontiers of piano. If Alfred Jaëll charmed the audience by his virtuoso and refined playing, Marie, by the depth of her touch, transported her listeners to a world beyond the piano. From then on Jeanne was bent on achieving exactly that kind of performance with her piano.

Yes, but how? The evening was over; Jeanne went home in ecstasy.

Between stays in Paris, the Jaëlls continued their untiring concert tours. They very soon became the most famous couple in the concert halls of Europe.

The history of music counts few artistic couples of such talent. Each one of them was famous, and what is more rare, each one was able to maintain his individual personality.

Alfred's playing was founded on charm and grace, while Marie's was qualified as masculine and powerful. Though different in style and character, they had a point in common. Both were pioneers with an avant-garde spirit. Together they contributed greatly to promoting the modern music of their time. In their programs they always included the works of great musicians like Beethoven, Brahms, Chopin, Liszt, Mendelssohn, Rubinstein, Saint-Saëns, and Schumann, who were responsible for leading the evolution of the piano, both as an instrument of soloists and as an instrument accompanying chamber music.

In the second half of the nineteenth century, Paris piano manufacturers, headed by Erard and Pleyel, were on the look out for leading pianists to play their latest models. Soon they recognized the qualities of both Alfred and Marie. Erard Manufacturers supplied pianos to Alfred as they had done for Liszt, a few years earlier. Marie chose to go with Pleyel, and she was a worthy ambassador. She also conducted joint research with Camille Pleyel, on the link between the pianist's touch and piano's mechanism.

The ever greater needs of the virtuosos stimulated the inventiveness of the great piano manufacturers. Indeed, during this time, the piano as an instrument evolved at breath-taking speed and rapidly acquired its final form.

Innovations in the mechanism of the piano were to influence and orient Marie Jaëll's future research on the art of touch and pedagogy; but, at the time, she had not the least inkling of her pedagogical vocation. However, a seemingly insignificant event occurred that had a lasting effect on her. It took place in Rome during one of the couple's visits.

Liszt stayed often in Rome — when he was not at Weimar or Budapest. With joy, he welcomed Alfred and Marie, who came to see him there in 1868. It was the first time Marie heard him play the piano. What happened to her was beyond description!

It was a profound revelation, an intense emotion, a shock that would overwhelm her and direct the entire course of her life. Years later she would recall the memorable moment:

> When I first heard Liszt play, in 1868, all my aural faculties seemed to be transformed at the instant the concert started. Such a transformation struck me much more than the playing itself. While I was listening to this music, so different from what I had heard till then, I felt my thoughts spin around as if they had acquired the capacity to move to and fro, independently of my will, by paths I did not suspect.[26]

Liszt's playing entranced Marie. But she hardly realized then that it was to become the central object of her research.

Why did his sounds leave such an impression on her? Probably because Liszt's nature, deep down, resembled hers, a soul ever in search of, and passionately in love with beauty. Both were persons of passion, drawn towards the same voyages of inner landscapes.

As a child, Liszt also loved to dream before the serene landscapes of his Hungarian countryside, to listen to bird songs and the droplets of light rain. He was enchanted by the music of bohemians and gypsies, those eternal wanderers, when every summer they descended from their caravans with gaudy costumes and danced to rustic melodies played on the violin or timbale.

In his own way, Liszt also bore the imprint of God's hand (or perhaps the Devil's, since the famous Italian music publisher Ricordi exclaimed after listening to him play, "*Questo è Liszt — o il Diavolo*"!).

"A young man who thinks a lot, who dreams, who delves into everything," people said of him in his youth. "His brain is as

---

26. *Les Rythmes du regard et la dissociation des doigts*, p.3

extraordinary as his fingers, and if he were not such a smart musician he would have been a philosopher."

Quite a few years later, it was no surprise to hear Liszt make the same comment about Marie Jaëll: "An artist's fingers and a philosopher's brain." Hence, it is not by chance that these two artists, filled with the same love of music, came to appreciate each other.

When she first heard him play, she instantly realized how much the manner of playing influences the listener. The way he played led her to discover another piano, another world, where music came alive in space and time.

But Marie was not the only one to have felt such emotion upon listening to Liszt. He was legendary; his playing captivated all music lovers.

Let us go back in time. Several years earlier, Clara Wieck, having listened to him for the first time in 1838 with her fiancé, a taciturn young man called Robert Schumann, wrote in her diary:

> We have heard Liszt... He cannot be compared to any other virtuoso. He evokes fright and wonder. He is a very lovable artist. His attitude at the piano cannot be described — he is original, he sinks before the instrument. His passion knows no limit. We can say of him, his art is his life...
>
> I began to sob, I was overwhelmed. My playing now seemed dull and inconsistent. Ever since I saw and heard the virtuoso play of Liszt, I have the impression of being a beginner.

Robert Schumann became lyrical.

> Too new, too powerful are our impressions for any balanced commentary to be possible. The breath of a genius is felt, and not described. When Liszt settles down at the piano, he first passes his hand through his hair, then his eyes become fixed, his chest calms down, his head and facial expressions reveal the sentiments he feels. I cannot describe how he played. It has to be heard.

MY ART IS A SCIENCE

In a modest way Marie Jaëll lived out "two nineteenth century myths, that of the artist as a Romantic hero, and that of the scientist as a seeker of truth."[27] Romanticism in music was in full bloom at the time she was born. She laid claim to what was sublime in it, and she remained a full-blooded but non-flamboyant Romantic throughout all her life. As she reached adulthood, the human and natural sciences were in a spectacular take-off. Self-educated, she became a quintessential pluralist and exploited the discoveries of science to probe the mysteries of piano music.

At a much deeper level, Marie Jaëll's piano pedagogy sought to transcend the apparent dichotomy of the Industrial Revolution and the Romantic Revolution that defined her epoch. During her life span, Europe underwent a total intellectual and spiritual overhaul. There was an explosion of creativity in all domains of human enterprise. Science and technology took giant steps forward. Industrialism started its triumphant march. General living standards rose continuously and a large middle class came to life. Truly, Western Europe gave birth to a new civilization. Such epoch-making changes provided the seedbed for Marie Jaëll's work.

The value-system that launched the revolutionary transformation was elaborated by the eighteenth century Enlightenment. Its roots go back to the "Awakening of Science" at the time of Renaissance. A conviction that harmony ruled the cosmos led to a search for the laws of symmetry underlying physical phenomena.

The founders of modern physics, like Galileo (1564-1642), Kepler (1570-1630) and Newton (1642-1727), believed in "the music of the spheres." Art and nature seemed to obey similar laws of harmony. Mersenne (1583-1648) hailed music as a beautiful part of mathematics. He even declared, "All science is art and all art is science," a belief that was close to Marie Jaëll's heart.

27.Morse

Newton's mechanics blossomed into modern science. Its spectacular success dealt a deathblow to earth-centered cosmology and undermined medieval theology. It also became the paradigm for all enquiries into the nature of man and of human societies. Descartes (1596-1650), Newton's contemporary, proposed a machinist view of the world. A confirmed dualist, he contended that body and soul were totally distinct, with the body considered morally inferior to the less material, more ethereal mind. His rationalist theory of innate ideas and description of nature in terms of machines and automatism were the dominant philosophy of the eighteenth century.

Following Descartes, the Philosophers of the "Age of Reason" undertook a systematic rationalization of all activity, and believed in human engineering to liberate man from oppression. They ordained that reason alone gave access to truth. They over-emphasized abstract reason and sanctioned the extension of automatism to all fields of human activity. They also argued that it was not within the reach of all. Thus they disdained the masses, mired, in their view, in the irrationality of religion. In their hands, reason became a critical tool of analysis allowing men to rid of their prejudices. Downgrading the symbolic social order inspired by religion, they wrote off the Church-dominated Middle Ages as Dark Ages. Their glorification of the economic man's individualism let him shed all social obligations. Their vision is summed up in the vague term Classicism.

There are several strands in Classicism. What holds them all together is the absolute belief in the capacity of the human reason to order this world, and dominate it. Inspired by Descartes, most Classicists attributed all form of movement, feeling and thought processes to the soul. Defenders of truth as clear and distinct ideas obtained through reason, they looked down upon sensory perception as an inferior animal process. The rationalist philosophers also subjected imagination and arts to the rule of reason.

With its concern for law, order and conformity, Classicism claimed to define the precise nature and exact limits of each of the arts. It decreed that balance, restraint, symmetry and wholeness must inform all art. Its conventions outlawed extravagance from artistic style so that it could express correctly proper shades of meaning rather than of feeling. In its view, art ought to be content to imitate nature. Immanuel Kant (1724-1804) summed up eighteenth century rationalist aesthetics by ranking instrumental music lowest among the arts.

In sharp contrast to Classical Greek literature, the works of the second half of the seventeenth and the first half of the eighteenth century shied away from revealing man's deeper emotional life. The Neo-Classical heritage was pushed to perfection even as the ideas of Romanticism were taking shape. Early French Romantic writers and artists like Victor Hugo (1802-1885), Lamartine (1790-1869), Berlioz (1803-1869) and Delacroix (1798-1863) were all born during the Revolutionary and Napoleonic era.

Thus as the nineteenth century unfolded, the deep cultural movement we call Romanticism surfaced as an antithesis to Classicism. It also harked back to the Renaissance discovery of the "individual" and proposed a new vision of art, and ranked music highest among the arts. Under its influence the world of music also changed, and by mid-nineteenth century, instrumental music in which piano held sway, moved to the center stage of musical life.

What, then, were the emergent forces at the close of the eighteenth century that pushed Romanticism to the fore? The defining event for nineteenth century Europe was the French Revolution of 1789, which exposed the turbulence of the deep social undercurrents. Its one rallying cry was "liberty." It swept away the *Ancien Regime*, the social hierarchy founded on birth. The hopes it raised and the terror it unleashed were to haunt the European consciousness for a long time. The accompanying turmoil let loose long pent-up forces in Europe.

With Napoleon's fall in 1815, the Bourbon monarchy was restored. The Revolution had failed to implement the greater portion of its declared program of Enlightenment. The propaganda of revolutionary France, carried across Europe by the force of arms, turned out to have left a legacy more of violence than of liberation. Thus the political ideas underlying the Revolution were corrupted, so that even the vocabulary that expressed them became suspect, and Enlightenment ideas fell into disrepute. Still, the rising middle classes, though a tiny minority of the population at the time, had taken over the public space and could not accept the return of the *Ancien Regime*. The society seemed to have lost its moorings. The visible economic and social dynamism was interwoven by bewildering and bloody changes of political regimes.

Romanticism first rose in Prussia between 1760 and 1830. It emerged there, Isaiah Berlin argues, because the Germans were losers, "a large collection of socially crushed and politically miserable human beings."[28] Since they could not compete with the French in social, political and philosophical accomplishments, they denied the importance of such things. Thus Romanticism took off as a triumph of the local and the humble over Enlightenment pretensions to universal truth. It always contained a streak of the irrational, along with an emphasis on unrestrained emotion and on dramatic conflict of contrasting elements. Its vision permeated literature a generation ahead of music — Goethe (1749-1832) dismissed the Romantic literature of his country as a disease!

Then, in 1815, France herself tasted military defeat. Many French Romantics were torn between a France of lost glory and dominion and a France of the imagination. They seemed to find solace in the sensuous wonders of the Orient and the mysteries of the Middle Ages. Curiously, humiliation on the battlefield did not seem to have dampened the French spirit. Indeed, during the nineteenth century the country was to lead Europe in intellectual, literary and artistic creativity. Paris became the largest, and culturally the richest, city in Europe. In music, after two centuries of

---

28.Berlin, Isaiah, *The Roots of Romanticism*, (ed. by Henry Hardy) Princeton University, 1999

Italian domination, it took up the leading role in the development of opera.

From the depth of such societal crisis, worsened by the repressive atmosphere of the Restoration, Romanticism in France asserted itself partly as a reaction against the dryness of Enlightenment rationalism and partly to integrate the new social energies rising to the surface. Firmly attached to the emancipation of the individual, it rejected the cold materialism of the mounting economic order. In its fight, it tried to join the emotional warmth of the people to the rationalism of the rising middle class intellectuals. It was to follow the trajectory of the material and spiritual upheaval overtaking Europe during the century. Its tenet that art and social action could make for a better world was to shift from optimism to pessimism as profit-driven industrial capitalism gained ground.

The Romantics very self-consciously stood on the threshold of a new movement in history. They refused to live under the long shadow cast by what they saw as soul-destroying rationalism. They aspired to re-create wonder in a world made narrow and prosaic by coldly linear Classicism. Truly Romanticism was Counter-Enlightenment.[29] In a sense, it was a revolt against the formal, the cold and the logical. It prefigured another sort of modernity.

As the century advanced, both science and art made spectacular breakthroughs, and their evolution was neither parallel nor linear. Unfortunately, the Romantic idealization of art was to create a misunderstanding that eventually ended in a divorce between art and science.[30]

Is there an exact definition of Romanticism? No sooner is it defined than it begins to dissolve. No body of doctrine sums it up definitively. A protean quality, continuously varying through time, hovers over it. Yet, in spite of constant change, a peculiar integrity informs it. Its great and unique contribution to modernity is its insistence that every human being is an inviolable absolute. It

---

29. Berlin I., Counter-Enlightenment, *History of Ideas.*

30. Changeux, *Raison et Plaisir*, p. 144

projected a new vision of man and nature, and transformed artistic life in Europe. Thus, it is best to view Romanticism as a movement to be explored.

The Romantics claimed total freedom for artistic creation. Following the French Revolution's cult of liberty, they turned their back on all norms. Nor were they in a hurry to propose a new set of norms. They only wanted to do away with the belief that one needs rules. "They fight for a progressive abolition of the hierarchy of genres and of the distinction between central and marginal forms."[31]

Romanticism in music, painting, literature or even philosophy is above all the celebration of the individual and, more pointedly, of the importance and value of individual "expression," whatever the norms and demands of society. It is the culture of radical individualism, one that puts more value on the inner feeling than the outer product, even in art. The Romantics stress the uniqueness of the artists' personal vision and the need to ground knowledge in the particular.

The Romantic thinkers and artists, though they were at odds with the Age of Reason on fundamental issues, never jettisoned the concept of reason. But they rejected the view that "reason is all" in human matters, and championed the individual and the particular against the Enlightenment universal. Their youthful excitement found outlets in the arts. Their search for meaning of the inner and outer life gave stimulus to life sciences like biology,[32] and social sciences like psychology.

The new artists were at pains to show that art, too, like reason, discloses truth, and that works of art are not created by the application of mechanical rules. They were all inspired by a cult of sensation and emotion. Above all, they dismissed the view that the vocation of art is to imitate nature. They felt that it was denigrating to man to sideline the dimension of his emotions. In their view,

---

31. Rosen, C., *The New York Review of Books*

32. Jacob, F., "Qu'est ce que la vie?" in *Université des Savoirs, (ed) Michaud* Y., Odile Jacob, Paris, 2000, p.23

reason, by itself, has no power to stimulate or motivate people to act, and art alone can inspire people.

The Romantics also made claims for a truth of the emotion and a belief in the freedom of the imagination. They found inspiration in the plenitude of life, and listened to the voices of the heart, often heard in forest solitude. They wanted to reconcile man and nature, and probed the links between the conscious and the unconscious. They reached out in new directions in search of light from all sources. They worked independently of one another, though in close knowledge of each other's work.

In stark contrast to the Cartesian machinist view, the Romantic vision views the universe as one great life and as an organic whole. It sees man in the context of great cosmic and historical movements that envelope him in an infinity greater than himself. Romantics challenge the idea of fixed insurmountable limits to human nature, a theme found in their omnipresent language of "boundary breaking." They are in search of new worlds, one inner, the other, outer. They are neither historians nor prophets. They are explorers of existence.

The first Romantics battled against atheism, and presented their program in religious terms. To them art and religion were closely intertwined and mutually supportive. Their discovery of religion was thus a discovery of the source of their art. Their movement could be seen as a rescue operation to salvage the debris of religion torn apart by science and Enlightenment. Indeed, the Romantics recovered the symbolic dimension of man highlighted by religion and gave it an acceptable secular form. They emphasized the emotional and universal aspects of religion against its ecclesiastical form. In their hands, the image of infinity took on a political significance

The Romantic man seeks the unity of his being. He asks spiritual questions, he wonders what reasons he can have to hope and to act in order to overcome his anguish and to give meaning to his life through his ever increasing knowledge and his earthly rooting. In a sense, infinite longing is the essence of Romanticism, though its concept of the infinite need not be the supernatural realm of theism.

The Romantics were highly self-conscious of their identity. All of them dealt explicitly with the nature of their art, and so formulated their own proper aesthetics. They argued that the different arts are but particular manifestations of the unique and mysterious principle of activity in its essence. Both art and religion draw their inspiration there. All over Europe there was a symbiosis among arts, poetry, painting and music. Great Romantic composers like Franz Schubert (1797-1828) and Robert Schumann (1810-1856) composed songs in abundance.

The Romantics hoped to achieve "immediacy" in the arts. Inheriting Rousseau's deep distrust of language, they wanted an art that speaks at once and to all. They planned to pull down all barriers between life and art. They looked for forms of expression that would be directly understandable without convention and without previous knowledge of tradition. Due to their drive, all Romantic art is permeated with instability and variability of meaning in style and action.

Thus, they struggled for a new freedom in the use of meaning. In their view there was no possibility of direct and authentic communication without some looseness and some play in the mechanics of language. The symbolic language the Romantics dreamt of, for art, was to be a natural one, not derived from the arbitrary conventions handed down by tradition. They dropped the aspects of the language of art that could be codified.

Thanks in part to the Romantics, the nineteenth century was also the golden age of sensory physiology and psychology. They brought the unconscious to the center stage of their concern. To them it was the locus of personal authenticity and the driving force of artistic creation. They called on natural philosophy to prove the unity of body and spirit, man and nature, the conscious and the unconscious, organism and environment. In their view symbolic thinking was a form of consciousness that extends beyond the here and now to a contemplation of the past and the future and a perception of the world. Thus, thinking and communicating through abstract symbols is the foundation of all creativity in art music and language.

Sigmund Freud (1856-1939), a founding father of modern psychology, probes the unconscious to make sense of the particular and original case of each human being. Along with Friedrich Nietzsche (1844-1900), he popularized the notion of the unconscious as the realm of the mind that controls human behavior. The new science of man would continue to grow in the hands of Freud's successors. Most outstanding among them was Carl Gustav Jung (1875-1961). His theory of symbolism shows how unconscious awareness plays a critical role in our experience of music.

Though sensibility and introspection became the surest basis for psychology, there were attempts to ground it on modern science. Alfred Binet's (1857-1911) "The Experimental Study of Intelligence," published in 1903, shows that intelligence is measurable in demonstrable capacity to respond critically to various types of selected stimuli. Helmholtz (1821-1894) a convinced materialist, tried to elucidate the physiology of perceptions, and organization of the mind. He fought the theory of "vitalism" that refused to reduce organism to non-organism and the living to physical and chemical reactions. He developed precise empirical theories of color and spatial perception. His "Physiological Psychology" is a physiological theory of music based on the study of auditory sensations. Late nineteenth century psychology emphasized the analogy between color and music.

Marie Jaëll would be inspired by this new knowledge of the unconscious in her research on the relations between man and art, and would trace the path that leads to the liberation of artistic expression. The unconscious that held her attention was the conceptual system underlying music to which human beings have no direct access. It is the cognitive unconscious, not repressed in the Freudian sense, but simply inaccessible to direct conscious introspection. In her vision of art, aesthetic intuition involves both conscious and unconscious activities.

The century also ushered in the machine age, with the attendant sweeping economic and social changes. The railways, visible symbols of the Industrial Revolution, made cheap and rapid travel available to the general public. Industry began to blacken the skies with soot. Radical political movements sprouted to organize the rising working class. Saint-Simonians spoke of an industrial civilization where the Romantic conscience would reign supreme.

The Industrial Revolution led to an urban revolution. Historians call the nineteenth century "the bourgeois century." With the spread of industrialism, the rising middle classes would take over the center stage. They adopted the life style and cultural practices of the former nobility, at least in part. Most of the musicians, like their contemporaries in painting and architecture, hailed from the growing ranks of the professional classes. The changed economic and social conditions underlay the growth of new cultural currents that sometimes coalesced into Romanticism.

In the meanwhile, European music moved out of private residences into concert halls, and became a platform art. Large cities developed a distinct corporative musical activity. Many of them boasted of public concert halls and conservatories. There was a rapid increase in the number of public concerts, and tastes tilted in favor of instrumental music. The musician at last emerged as an independent, versatile artist. He could now count on the enormous increase in the numbers and resources of the bourgeoisie and on the support of paying audiences. His financial security gave him intellectual independence, and he freely expressed his opinions.

Romantic music found its supreme expression in piano. Since a modern technological base was needed for its manufacture, Western Europe (soon to be followed by the U.S.A.) became the home to the new keyboard instrument.

The piano, delicate and powerful, mellow and full of tone color, was the preferred instrument of the new musicians. The Romantics sought inspiration from the depths of nature but gave voice to it through the new instrument. They all composed at the piano, for the piano; and then they played the piano. Berlioz, to whom music was the first of arts, put instrumental music at the center of all music.

Beethoven (1770-1827) had already marked the transition from music as performance to music as text, from the performer-composer known of the eighteenth century to the genius creator postulated by the nineteenth century. Texts composed for fluid performances and passed on from master to student over the ages evolved into documents to be written and read, and eventually were transformed into digitally-recorded artifacts. The idea also grew that interpretative artists had a right to freedom of expression through other artists' music.

The piano became central to musical life. It asserted its supremacy over the harpsichord for use in public halls. Its music became increasingly the pleasure of a cultured elite. The organ, ideologically as well as physically tied to the Church, lost its dominance as the secularized middle classes thronged to concert halls. The piano music was turned into a performance process that lay at the heart of the constitution of the new middle class society,[33] and was turned into a kind of lay liturgy. It inherited features of religiously ordered events like concentration and stillness. This explains the extreme attentiveness of audiences at concerts of classical music.[34]

"Music became democratic." True, composers after 1800 still deferred to the taste of patrons, but they wrote for the public whose growth fostered larger ensembles and longer compositions. As the fortunes of the aristocracy declined, the forces of supply and demand took over the art market. The publishing houses found that music could be profitable. The printing of music became a business in itself. Copies of the most admired music began to come within the reach of even the modest, who could make a living by performing for a public that was ready to pay, and by the sale of

33. Seeger A., *Music and Dance*, in *Companion Encyclopedia of Anthropology*, (ed) T. Ingold, p.689.

34. Gombrich, *The New York Review of Books*, March 4, 1993

sheet music to the general public. Chopin (1810-1849) lived off the profits of his publications and the proceeds of his lessons. The growing sources of income emancipated musicians from their dependence on royal and noble patronage. Such was to be the case of Marie Jaëll, who, as we have seen, was not born to wealth.

The piano also began to invade the parlors and drawing rooms of middle class families, and became a sign of social distinction and elegance. It symbolized bourgeois respectability, and was at the center of social change. Among the growing middle class, there was also a vast expansion of musical literacy, that is, the ability to hear a piece of music in an appropriate way, acquired intuitively through listening to it. On the other hand, there was a general eagerness for musical knowledge, reflecting the progress of musical interest of the middle class public. A piece of music came to be seen not as a collection of discrete sounds in progression but as a whole, held together by an overarching rhythmic unity. Most of all, the devotees of music were moved by the gestural and emotional content of what they saw and heard.

Another result of the Romantic Movement was the development of competing theories of aesthetics of art. "Musical science is also a child of the Romantic era."[35] Most Romantic artists, like Delacroix and Baudelaire, were theoreticians of their art. Berlioz was a tireless writer and was a leading factor in the evolution of the ideas of Romanticism. Musical scholarship and learning expanded brilliantly during the second half of the century. Another outstanding feature of the era was the growth of musical journals. A remarkable increase in the publication of guides to musical theory, in the form of popular textbooks of all kinds, furthered the trend.

This "rebellious" century, deeply unsettled by nationalisms, wars, discoveries, and undercurrents of the heart and soul, refuses to be pigeonholed in rationalist categories. Similarly Romanticism, a truly pan-European movement, fails to fit into an intellectual straitjacket. It changes its nature, following different epochs and

---

35.Einstein Alfred, *Romanticism in Music*, p.416

countries. It is above all a state of the mind, in search of material expression. What is certain is that as a great movement of thought it had a capital influence on piano art and musical language, artistic realization and on the way of being an artist.

The new social, cultural and technical universe forms the background to Marie Jaëll's research. By 1850, many of the Romantic attitudes had become respectable. Her encounters, readings, musical culture, and travels have all enriched her natural Romantic spirit. She would spend the greatest part of her life wondering about the state of artist's conscience in search of authentic expression in the context of revolutionary changes. All her work pulsated with the activities and concerns of writers, scientists, philosophers and musicians of her era. Her aesthetics of music and her pedagogy were attempts at reconciling the twin heritage of Classicism and Romanticism through piano music.

She claimed repeatedly that her art was a science. She did not add that "honorific term" so that her method could partake of the prestige then attached to physics; her ambition was to obtain a systematic and rational knowledge of the best piano technique. She would never dream of reducing music, with its "undifferentiated awareness and mystical experience," to scientific laws.

From the Heart, Let It Speak to the Heart

Thus prayed Beethoven, in his manuscript of the *Missa Solemnis*. His wish sums up the Romantic vision of music. "All Western music leads up to him and all Western music leads away from him." He was one of the first composers to introduce Romantic themes into music. His feeling for nature was uncommonly profound, and all his life he sought the open air. Troxler, one of the first Swiss Romantic philosophers, who knew him personally, observed, "By force of feeling and thinking, of wanting and working, I can reach an infinite depth in me where I find I am face to face with myself."

According to a Marxist view (as put forward by Adorno), Romantic music arose as a protest against the growing reification of capitalist culture. It is true that the great composers imposed their often uncompromising subjectivity upon the traditional language of music.[36] The nineteenth century, mother of so many revolutions, is redeemed by the drama lived out by artists of the epoch. Indeed, a tragic destiny seemed to rule over many Romantic artists, who died young or wrote themselves out at an early age. It was as if the poets, painters and composers faltered when confronting the revolutionary breakthroughs in science and industry. Marie Jaëll suffered similar tensions as she tried to create a niche for herself in a male-dominated universe.

The fascination evoked by the term Romanticism comes from the music it inspired. The foremost composers who came to be called Romantic were born around 1810: Car Maria von Weber (1786-1826), Berlioz, Liszt (1811-86), Schubert, Mendelssohn (1809-1847), Chopin and Schumann. In their hands, pure instrumental music, the most abstract of the arts, reached the heights of sublime. Their drive led them to find in music direct expression of emotion devoid of concepts. To them, musical sounds were symbols of communion with fellow beings.

The Romantic composers unhesitatingly exploited music as a form of emotional self-projection. Beethoven, as his hearing worsened, increasingly turned to music as a means of direct communication to break through his isolation. His *Pastoral Symphony* is "more an expression of feeling than a painting," though its thought content harks back to Classicism. His most characteristic masterpieces revel in the dramatic intensity of his soul and not of the theater. His later works opened the floodgates to the Romantic music of composers like Berlioz and Schumann.

The spirit of Romanticism is at its most appealing in Schumann's piano music. He created a musical technique that

---

36. Rosen, C., "Should We Adore Adorno," *The New York Review of Books*, October 24, 2002, p. 2.

allowed his art to assume the function of literature without taking on a literary meaning and without losing its status as music. Berlioz also caused elements of musical form to bear meanings analogous to verbal ones. Thanks to them, the ability of music to create meaning and significance out of its elements without any attempt to mirror the outside world became the model for other arts.

For a long period, instrumental music had played a subsidiary role to vocal music. But all the Romantics — poets, painters and novelists — hailed it as the ideal art, the greatest and deepest of arts. They were convinced that it unlocked the door to their chosen realm of faith. They all acclaimed the divinity of music that helps people get a glimmer of contact with the supernatural. To them, the musician was a priest, the sole figure capable of deciphering the hieroglyphs of nature.

For all of Vienna's pre-eminence, the world capital of the new movement was Paris. Romanticism in France reached articulate expression in literature and painting at least a generation earlier than in music. In literature, the beginning of the century saw a reaction against classical conventions. Its main proponents were Victor Hugo, Vigny, Lamartine and Musset. They sought a greater freedom of language and gave a new emphasis on sentiments and emotions.

Chateaubriand (1768-1848) embodied the new spirit. His books, composed in musical prose, exerted a great influence on young poets, writers and artists. When the youthful Liszt discovered him, he fell, like so many others, under the bewitching spell of this charmer who brought to life the forgotten poetry of Christianity. Concerning him, the pianist loved to repeat, "on love and religion, the two eternally vibrant strings that resound simultaneously in mankind, he has unlocked heavenly harmonies that hold hearts captive."

Soon Romanticism was to become a torrent fed by multiple streams. It drew on romance, imagination, mysticism, the strange, the picturesque and the fantastic. It was fired by a new vision of religion, and the passion of love. The "rediscovery" of the Middle Ages inspired artists, particularly the painters. Delacroix, the foremost Romantic painter, was entranced by visions of medieval décor and atmosphere. In one of his paintings, "The Alchemist's," he mixes together helter-skelter all of Faust's philters of supernatural curiosities and the quirks of Gothic architecture.

The Romantics, in their search for authenticity, believed in the journey inwards. Thanks to them, the new century allowed man to rediscover his soul, and therefore God — and also the Devil. They were obsessed with the complex nature of evil. Mephistopheles provided unending inspiration to artists who were prey to diverse doubts. Their hero was Faust, in whom Romantic ideals for humanity alternated with bouts of frank sensuality. His bargain with Mephistopheles underscores the key Romantic theme of striving for the infinite.

Faust's story inspired Berlioz, Charles Gounod (1818-1893), Schubert and Liszt to some of the finest and most characteristic music of the epoch. His temptations, questionings, hopes and despairs were immortalized by Goethe and illustrated in 1820 by Delacroix's bizarre and exciting lithographs. The painter was fascinated by the drama where the human mind is confronted with its enigmas, and the human heart faces its desires. The devil leads the dance, and Faust and Mephistopheles enter the Sabbath night on fiery horses, an image that always haunted Delacroix. Liszt himself, become Abbé, would write several Mephistopheles waltzes, dedicating the third one to Marie Jaëll.

The Romantics were also haunted by the themes of suffering transfigured into beauty, and disenchantment sublimated into art. As Marie Jaëll said, in her journal,

> We cannot escape the law of suffering, but we must suffer in order to triumph — we must not suffer to succumb. Anguish saps strength, if it does not lead to action....Art, what splendor! Vibrating in contact with universal harmony.
> Oh, human sufferings, what is left of you in such moments? You disappear...the soul opens itself up to infinite beauty, and dis-

cerns the soaring heights that are hidden from the eye. It approaches God.[37]

Romanticism also marked the return of the repressed classes, for artists discovered the social implications of their art — or, rather, of their profession as artists. They became convinced that paths of art and knowledge must free mankind from material misery and lead to the discovery of the beauty of sounds and colors. The novels of George Sand and Victor Hugo sympathetically portrayed the life of lower orders. They broke with the restricted world to which their creativity had been confined. Convinced that high culture must be thrown open to the masses, they declared art to be the sole repository of spiritual values, the salvation of the nation and the family of humankind. The Classicists and the Romantics were on a collision course.

The first open conflict between the proponents of the old and the new artists took place at the Painting Exhibition in Paris in 1827. "The whole world of painting is on the warpath," wrote Delacroix, "and everyone who wields a palette is rushing to get to the front on time. The models are all in a tizzy, and the pigment salesmen just smile and smile. It seems that the members of the jury are going to go after any innovation like a pack of dogs."

The cultural atmosphere exuded an air of revolt, provoked and kept alive by the younger generation. At the famous "battle of Hernani" on February 25, 1830, longhaired costumed adolescents, with Berlioz among them, took the *Théâtre Français* by storm to "tonsure the head of Classicism" and cheered Victor Hugo's "Hernani" on opening night. They announced a cultural revolution. Romantic, literary and social revolts at last joined hands. They had a vision of infinite social improvement.

The Revolution of 1830 prompted Victor Hugo, Lamartine and Lammenais to compose hymns to the new spirit of freedom and celebrate the downfall of Absolutism. Delacroix commemorated the

---

37. Jaëll, Marie, Journal (unpublished)

event by painting "Liberty Leading the People," a masterpiece in which a young working-class woman is seen leading a crowd in protest against an oppressive regime. There is Classicism in the figure of Liberty, but Romanticism in the restlessness and Realism in the details. He thus illustrates the intense preoccupation of the social Romantics to forge political and cultural links between the high and the low in France. "The social Romantics of the July Monarchy represent a rupture with the centuries-old tendency of the elite culture to distance itself disdainfully from the popular culture."[38] This Revolution threw the aristocracy out of the center of musical patronage.

Soon, Paris took up arms to overthrow political despotism. Charles X, King of France, fled abroad. Louis-Philippe assumed the title of "King of the French." Liszt even dreamt of composing a symphony of the Revolution.

The Revolution of 1848 marked the high tide of Romanticism in politics. "It was the springtime of the peoples," but was unfortunately nipped in the bud by a confluence of the Russian, Austrian and Prussian Empires. In 1852, France herself became an Empire, proclaimed by Napoleon III. The Empires became the bulwarks of the *Ancien Regime*, even as industrialism began sapping their roots.

The lure of distant lands drew painters and poets like Chateaubriand, Victor Hugo, Lamartine and Delacroix to visit Italy, Greece and countries of the Near East, where they sought to recover the innocence of a bygone age. They hoped to find there a certain escape from the traditions that stifled them at home.

Chateaubriand visited the Holy Land and North Africa in 1806. Victor Hugo soon followed him. His drawings as well as his poetry evoke in the wondrous landscapes of his travels. In 1832, Delacroix left for Morocco, and brought back his wonderful paintings in violent colors. For the rest of his life, he was to draw on the wealth

---

38. Mitzman A. Michelet

of experience and imagery accumulated during his four months stay there.

The Romantics made Italy the land of their choice. It attracted them all by its picturesque scenes, verve, and harmony. Poets like Byron, Keats, Gautier and Musset extolled this country of enchantment. Nietzsche himself wrote, "Every time we look around, there is something great and new to see."

Delacroix, Romantic painter *par excellence*, was also the most scholarly artist of his age. He always insisted that he was also a Classicist, and held Ingres (1780-1867) in high esteem. He sought a synthesis of Romanticism and Classicism, and tried to re-appropriate the grand tradition of mural painting.

He had a disdain for academic rectitude. As a painter of passions, he took great liberties with drawing. In his writings he is eloquent on the forces that inspired him. In his journal he noted, "God is within us; it is this inner presence which makes us admire the beautiful, which heartens us when we have done well. It is this that inspires men of genius and stirs them when they contemplate their own achievements."[39] The poetry of sacred texts fired his imagination.

He favored any technical device that led to greater warmth. In his paintings, color and distribution of light are essential. Through specific pictorial techniques, he invested his paintings with expressive movement that conveys to the viewer the emotions that inspired him. His wonderful chords of color often give one the ideas of melody and harmony. Indeed, through color his paintings become music and express their aspiration towards the infinite. Baudelaire hailed Delacroix as the artist of the inner world, and called his paintings musical.

He was a leader of the colorist school in the war between drawing and color. His great achievement was the fusion of color and line. His work transforms landscape into a vehicle of the sublime for the expression of feelings without losing its existence as

39. Gage, John. *Color and Culture*, p 235.

pure landscape. In his view, "a painter saves on paint when he owns brushes of truth."

As a colorist, his influence on the Impressionists was to be profound. From his work they became aware of mutability as an ever-present reality, and the need to enjoy natural beauty while it lasted. His influence on the techniques of painting was to grow, while his Romanticism found less support among the rising generation.[40] Van Gogh, his most devoted follower, contended that a work of art must be an expression of inner life, and not a slavish imitation of nature.

Nineteenth century painters were friends of composers and performers of music. They also viewed themselves as performers and they used their own very ample experience to illuminate their practice as visual artists. Delacroix argued that all art aspires to the condition of music, since a composer is supremely free. In collaboration with Chopin, he elaborated the idea that the liaison between musical notes, "the logic of their succession" and what he called their "aural reflections" were a precise parallel to the reflection of colors in nature and painting.

Liszt was a key figure of nineteenth century music, along with Berlioz Chopin, Schumann, and Brahms. "His seventy-five year life span tidily envelops Romanticism in music so that he seems to reign over it."[41] He belonged to the band of Romantic artists among whom are found Chateaubriand, whose books he devoured, Lamartine whom he admired, De Vigny, Lammenais, Victor Hugo, Delacroix, and many others who spanned the century with him. He kept copies of Goethe's *Faust* and Dante's *Inferno* in every room of his residence.

All the artists in their own way embodied the Europe of the time, in full creative explosion. Writers, musicians and painters fraternized and, intoxicated with the ideals of liberty and Romanticism, remade the world according to their dreams.

---

40. Cage
41. Cairns

Liszt also decided to leave for Italy in 1836, to discover the landscapes that endlessly fascinated the Romantics. He traveled with Marie d'Agoult, with whom he had been living for three years. Rich, young, elegant and aristocratic, Marie d'Agoult had opened a Parisian salon where Rossini played, Malibran sang and where Liszt and Chopin later performed. She met Liszt in 1836 in the salon of a marquise; they began a liaison that became stormy over the years and ended in bitterness. Marie d'Agoult has left us a flamboyant portrait of the young Liszt during their first meeting. He was 22.

> The door opened, and a curious appearance offered itself to my eyes. I say appearance, for lack of a better word, to render the extraordinary sensation caused by the most extraordinary person I had ever seen. Tall and excessively slender, a pale face, big sea-green eyes which sparkled quick gleams similar to a wave when it is ablaze, a sickly and powerful countenance, an indecisive walk which seemed to glide rather than pose on the ground, distracted air, anxious, and like a ghost to whom the hour sounds to return into darkness. That was how I saw before me that young genius whose hidden life awakened lively curiosities as his triumphs had formerly evoked jealousy.

A few months later Marie d'Agoult abandoned her graying husband, and even her children, to elope with the young musician to Switzerland, where they would live for a while. The Parisian salons would pardon her, with difficulty.

On their way to Italy, Lamartine hosted the two lovers at the outset of their journey, in Burgundy, in a lofty medieval manor surrounded by several acres of woods. Moved by his meeting with the great poet, whom he admired so much, Liszt sat down at Madame de Lamartine's piano one evening and played his étude, "*harmonie du soir*," an exquisite piece dedicated to Lamartine himself.

The memorable evening inspired the great poet to some passionate lines:.

> The young Liszt, with his magical fingers, tossed his spontaneous and supernatural symphonies to the wind. Only a breeze

could have composed such vagabond improvisations, disheveled as the lovely blond head of this Hoffmann of music... The notes just touched our hearts impressionistically when the artist was improvising at the piano in the salon, for hours, with candles extinguished, windows open and curtains floating in the moonlight. The puffs of night air, blowing in from the meadows, carried the airborne melodies to the astonished echoes of the woods and streams.

Liszt and his companion visited Italy as pilgrims during the fall of 1838 and the winter of 1839. The country enchanted the musician and fired his imagination. From his voyage he would bring back nearly five hundred pages of music, rich in new harmonies, colors and virtuosity.

Overwhelmed by so much expression of beauty, Liszt wrote to Berlioz, "Raphaël and Michelangelo made me better understand Mozart and Beethoven. Fra Beato Angelico explained Allegri to me. Titian and Rossini seemed to me two similar stars. The Coliseum and the Campo Santo are not so unfamiliar, as one may think, to the Heroic Symphony and the Requiem... and Michelangelo will find perhaps one day his musical expression in a Beethoven of the future."

Later he would write, "I am perhaps a failed genius. Only time will tell. I feel I am hardly a mediocre person. My own mission is to be the first to have put poetry in the music of the piano with some brilliance. I attach the highest importance to my harmonies."

A few years later Marie Jaëll would fall prey to similar anxieties. She had imbibed the Romantic world vision, for she was educated both in heart and soul by the century in which she lived. Like Liszt, she would ask the same fundamental questions on art, its mission and its deep links with man.

"Why do philosophical ideas pursue me everywhere?"[42]

"I just cannot be simply an artist."

42.Jaëll, Marie, Journal (unpublished)

The spirit changes meaning and dimension. Man ceases to obey only the laws of logical mechanism of thought and reason. The most intimate regions of nature are awakened by this nascent sentimentalism, this mystical renewal.

In a Europe where uprisings and tyrannies begin to produce generations of refugees, exile provided a political theme. "Exile is not a material thing, it is a moral thing," proclaimed Victor Hugo, from the Isle of Jersey, where he withdrew after Napoleon's self-proclamation as Emperor in 1852.

Both Liszt and Chopin, the leading pianists of the time, hailed from the heart of Central Europe. Their music is deeply bound to the political life of their countries, Poland and Hungary. Romantic music reached unprecedented heights of expression in Chopin's mazurkas and polonaises. He adopted and glorified national rhythms in his compositions, and became a heroic patriot.

In a book dedicated to the memory of his friend and sometimes rival, Liszt wrote,

> Chopin will be ranked among the top musicians who have personified within themselves the political sense of a nation through the rhythm of Polish mazurkas and krakowiaski, and he has given these names to many of his writings. He has therefore given all his pieces a life. All his works are held together by a unity. Both their beauty and shortfalls are always the consequences of the same order of emotion of an exclusive way of feeling. This is indeed the first condition of a poet, so that his songs make people vibrate in union with all the hearts of his motherland. What seduces the imaginations of every country is this gift of reproducing in a political formula the indefinite contours of rare sentiments that the national artists recognize and often encounter among their compatriots.

The nineteenth century witnessed the rise of nationalities; "popular" also means "national." During this era of popular awakening, artists, especially musicians, were at home in all the countries of Europe.

Musically, Liszt embodied Romantic Europe. His travels across the continent enriched his repertoire with folk rhythms, the chimes of village bells, romances, fluid Venetian barcarolles, vibrating Neapolitan tarantellas, and the languor and frenzy of gypsy improvisations. Every European nation, especially those under a foreign yoke like Ukraine, Poland and the Caucasus, but also Hungary, Italy, and Spain, has a niche in his music. Where there was a national cause to be defended, where man is under menace, his generous heart beat stronger and faster.

The Franco-Prussian war of 1870 came as a shock to European artists. Liszt succumbed to sadness, dismay, and embarrassment. He was French at heart, and admired Napoleon III and his Liberal Empire. His son-in-law Wagner was the musical symbol of the new Germany. He found himself hemmed in from all sides.

Marie Jaëll acknowledged that she felt closer to the German than the Latin genius. She had given her first concerts in Germany. Its music was her life. The war of 1870 for her was heart-rending. It pitted Germany, which had given her so much, against France and especially Alsace, her homeland. The French defeat inflicted a wound on her patriotic soul.

"Even now," she lamented, "I have not succeeded in shaking off this sadness that overwhelms me. Decidedly my heart is not made for so much hatred, and it pains me to foster anti-Christian and anti-human sentiments in my heart. Still, I try to reconcile patriotism with pardon, to turn ill-feeling into charity; but alas!, fully absorbed in my pain I always see these foreigners in our plains, towns, homes; I see my country bleeding, and we all, her children, are living in exile!"

A little later she wrote to Liszt:

> Dear master, after endless struggles I have hit on a solution, not a solution of the reason but a solution of the heart. Reason creates nothing, it states; while the heart has the power to create something that was not there yesterday. Yesterday I wrote in German, today I write in French, and I have finally the courage to be of

one piece, to let blood flow smoothly from the roots to the flow-ers.[43]

That same year, Alfred Jaëll was asked if he would be willing to succeed Moshelés at the Conservatory of Leipzig and also to assume the direction of the musical journal founded by Schumann. He turned down the offers when the French defeat was announced. In the meantime, the Jaëlls had left for Switzerland, where they spent the war months. There they ran into Richard Wagner and Cosima. The two couples felt estranged by their conflicting sentiments of patriotism and offended each other violently.

Marie Jaëll and Wagner never got on well with each other.

The sentiments of nationalism grew powerfully during the nineteenth century. Little by little, they invaded the world of art. In 1871, Camille Saint-Saëns founded "*La Société Nationale de Musique*" and gave it the motto "*Ars Gallica*" to make clear its objective of freeing French music from German influence.

In the meanwhile, French poetry broke loose from the confines of classical prosody. Now, French versification had not undergone significant modification since the end of the sixteenth century. New poets like Baudelaire (1821-67), Verlaine (1844-96) and Mallarmé (1842-98) inaugurated a revolution in poetry.

Baudelaire proclaimed that the subject of poetry is inner life. His poems present an ontological image of symbols, rhythms and sounds. Verlaine also gave primacy to sensation in the representation of the exterior world while revealing the inner drama through rhythmic expressions. Mallarmé wanted poetry to express the idea of a transcendental world and to approach the abstraction of music. Indeed, his poems, when stripped of their oratorical art, become music without instruments.

The new poems were a spontaneous overflow of feeling. They also penetrated into the secrets of nature. They are filled with sensory images, colors, sounds and scents. "Painting is silent poetry,

---

43. M. Jaëll's letter to Liszt, date unknown

poetry is painting that speaks." Like the painters, the poets also hailed music as the ideal art, and they highlighted the relationship between painting and music by fixing a moment in the duration, and thus opened the way to French composers like Fauré and Debussy.

In the Romantic scale of values, music is given the pride of place among the arts. All describe musical creation as the volcanic eruption of a glowing soul in the grip of ecstatic revolution. "It is an activity engendered by enthusiasm, fire, imagination, and above all by the ability to feel, and feel passionately." According to the Romantics, music satisfied most readily and completely their aspirations towards the infinite, since the very essence of music is to be the expression of the infinite. Their claims were based on music's emotional appeal and its ability to take the listener out of himself. They believed that it could free the individual from the narrowness of existence, and takes the listener on a long mysterious journey.

Berlioz made special claims for music in terms of its emotional appeal and its ability to take the listener out of himself. His work was a powerful symbol of the true spirit of Romanticism, not only self-projecting but doing so on a scale larger than life. According to him, music offered a passport to another world; it was a shattering breakthrough of subjectivity. Liszt and other composers recreated literature in music.

"The French have no music."[44] This was Rousseau's observation in 1753. He was right, since French songs at that time were set to a musical style that was fundamentally Italian or German, and sounded false. Perhaps it did not occur to the musicians that the rhythms of spoken French, German and Italian are different. Spoken French is syllable-timed, in contrast to stress-timed German and Italian. It does not cause vowel decay, since all syllables are delivered with roughly equal value. In French, the stress always comes on the final syllables of words and phrases. In a short phrase, there is usually just one stress, as though the phrase

44. Monelle, R.

49

was one long, multi-syllable word. This absence of a strong stress and the irregular spacing of final stress, caused by the unequal length of phrases and words, gave some people the impression that French was fundamentally unmusical. The new poets, by indulging in rhythmic freedoms and arbitrary caesuras, broke through such misguided traditional views to create something new.

The union of music and poetry was one of the earliest and most remarkable phases of the Romantic Movement. At first, music was an essential partner in literary progress. Liszt took for his motto: "Renew music by joining it to poetry." Berlioz had already exploited the flexible rhythmic structure of the French language, with great flair. During the 1840s, he observed that the alliance between literature and music was flowering into symphonic poems. An arch-Romantic, his music was filled with images, at times macabre and supernatural, of nature. Liszt and his disciples recreated literature in music. Schumann brought about a union of instrumental music and poetry. Chopin was called the poet of the piano.

Soon, the masterpieces of Baudelaire, Verlaine and Mallarmé were set to new French music. Debussy, Fauré and Ravel, all of whom were under the spell of Liszt's virtuosity and splendor, came to be inspired by the new poets. Debussy introduced a new fluidity of forms and exploited the contrast of firm on-beat rhythms with floating effects, welding the strong beat and indulging in irregularities like triplets and duplets. He also espoused new fingering techniques at the piano that heretofore had been considered extravagant.

Debussy's music is the aural version of impressionist painting. By cultivating a way of seeing, he achieved a translucent, suggestive and complex musical language of feeling whose novel character may have derived from visual models. His new musical aesthetics embodied the eminently French qualities of moderation, elegance and clarity.

Destiny seems to have marked a clear trail for Marie Jaëll in her life's work. Everything seemed to be at hand when she began her career as a pianist. All the revolutionary ideas in diverse fields were to find a place in her theory of musical aesthetics. She would draw on the new wealth of knowledge as she embarked towards the end of the century on her self-given mission of developing piano pedagogy inspired by Liszt's approach. While developing her highly original pedagogy, she would seek to give it a scientific grounding.

While her encounter with Liszt planted the seeds that would sprout, grow into a plant and eventually blossom, she first passed through (after her marriage and in spite of an artistically rich life when her talents shone) a period of doubts and questionings. These never left her in peace.

Indeed, as Delacroix noted, "Truth is revealed only to genius, and genius is ever lonely." And Nietzsche added, "Genius is endless patience, and infinite striving or effort." In sum, more than anything else, single-mindedness is the true hallmark of the highest genius. Marie Jaëll's personality bore the trace of such qualities.

CAN A WOMAN, CALLED TO CREATE, BE A WIFE?

After their wedding, Alfred and Marie settled down to a comfortable life. They moved from country to country so often that they were nicknamed the traveling duo. After the Franco-Prussian War of 1870, however, Marie refused to visit Germany for some time. In 1872, when the Alsatians were given a choice, she opted for French nationality without hesitation and her husband, out of love for her, did the same. They gave regular concerts as soloists in Paris. They also participated in the great Parisian orchestras that were coming to life at the time, like Pasdeloup's "Concerts Populaires" (classical music) and Colonne's "Concerts de Châtelet."

Alfred was close to his wife; he doted on her, but could easily be provoked to jealousy. As for Marie, she came into her own, and her independent and full personality began to assert itself. This led to some clashes. But she sincerely admired her husband, reciprocated his affection, and desired to make him happy.

"One of the most fervent prayers I address to God," she wrote
to her mother, "is that He grants me the grace to make Alfred happy.
That would be the most effective consolation for my sufferings."

What are the sufferings she speaks of?

Her correspondence from those days gives us an inside view of
the questioning and doubts she felt so intensely, all inside herself,
confiding them only to intimate friends in her letters.

> I am always anxious about the work I must take up [she wrote
> to her sister]. My playing satisfies me only at long intervals, and
> then, only in fragments, rarely as a whole. I am always discovering
> my lacunae.
>
> ...To feel small in relation to what one wants to be, and to feel
> too great in relation to what one has achieved, to be torn between
> these two alternatives, without finding a solution, without find-
> ing the means to put an end to this state of struggle, to see always
> the task unfinished, to feel the soul burn with a fire that consumes
> it and to find it always unquenched, and to realize the human
> inability to abate this inner glow, this simmering volcano.
>
> ...Sometimes I am afraid, the excess of my sentiments frightens
> me. I wonder what I may become, if this lava that makes me trem-
> ble when it is held back happened to break through, if it became a
> torrent and made itself master of me?
>
> ...Oh! I am weak, for I am afraid of myself, but there is a more
> dangerous thing than to fear oneself; it is not to know oneself.

Marie was clear-headed. She sensed that something was at
work in her inmost depths that she could not yet fathom clearly. She
wished to play better or, rather, play differently, in an authentic
way.

"I have to play this evening; will my soul be at my fingertips?"

Later on, she take to composing with equal passion, hoping to
find, in her search for new harmonies, the means of abating her inner
flames, the volcano that was ready to burst forth but that had yet to
find its way.

Her diary reveals inner struggles that ran through her entire
being. She was deeply absorbed in herself, but with lucidity and

perspicacity. Peace and anxiety, enthusiasm and despair, doubts and convictions followed each other. The problems of life, of good and evil, of women, of love — and of creation — tormented her with equal intensity. She felt that "Art is One," that it cannot be shared nor subjected.

Can a woman whose destiny is to create, love? The question haunted her, and she could not yet find an answer to it — she who was so relaxed on other matters: "To be a woman and to be someone is almost impossible."

Several years later, in 1914, Catherine Pozzi, a public figure and author of poems and essays, was to claim that the fact that their author was a woman was one of the main obstacles to the dissemination and acceptance of Marie Jaëll's ideas. "Alsace, when it was French, produced a genius it does not yet know. A woman." These two words weighed heavily, alas, on Marie Jaëll's work; for a long time they were reason enough for those who could have understood her not to read her books.

"Art creates needs that cannot be dispensed with," she wrote. "One has to struggle to win freedom."

In her dismay, Marie sought advice from her friend Edouard Schuré:

> From a woman, gifted or not, man takes away everything, little by little, and robs her of her creative forces; he takes her life from her. How often I have seen my dreams shattered by this single fact. The union of two beings can certainly be beautiful, splendid, marvelous, but... Must a woman always give in, and make the choice between the wings of the body and the wings of the soul, sacrifice the former for the latter. Can't she keep all four? It is a mystery, and I wanted to see how it ends. Was the dream too reckless?

Schuré replied to her:

> If I understand you correctly, you wonder if love and art can go together, if the former is the enemy or friend, inspirer or destroyer of the latter. There is hardly a more serious or more complicated question. Wanting to solve it in general seems to me to be a pipe-dream since it varies entirely according to circumstances and nature. The realm of Eros is as infinite as that of life. It contains all

the depths and all the heavens. Two burning and self-aware hearts, who penetrate each other and are united to each other, can make their love a source of strength, faith and activity in spite of obstacles, trials, struggles that are nameless and endless.

I think I can claim that true passion is far more dangerous for the woman than for the man. The man usually seeks in it nothing but possession. The woman — I mean the one who loves truly — is absorbed, abandons herself, loses almost fatally her distinct individuality unless she finds sovereign moral support in the one whom she loves, which is rare.

Love is the greatest source of inspiration, the only true one I know. But if passion takes the upper hand, one may as well wave good-bye to art and creation. If you tell me, dear Ariel [his pet name for her], that you can fly better with what you call your four wings, I will tell you, boldly spread all four, and take off. But if you tell me that there is lead in one pair, I reply to you, sever it if you want to retake your flight, since it will grow again one day. The other pair is worth the trouble, surely, and it will take you far, I am sure.

I hope you are better, and you will soon recover two precious things: harmony with yourself, and clear awareness of what you want.

Don't you believe [Marie replied to him], that, in spite of myself, the only path I can take is one of privation?

I felt the disastrous influence of too powerful a sentiment; that is enough for me. To tell you the truth, I struggle with my body to free myself; I want to be fully and wholly to myself; I must triumph, and I give up the idea of living for someone else. The needs of my art create a life that I ought not to forsake. The world of my affections gets shrunk, so that, without doubt, I am not held back from my goal. It is only in progress that there is life for me.

Formerly, my dear friend, I fused the human being with the artist's; my art was produced in half by the woman's enthusiasm and pains. I was doubly inspired by earth and heaven. From earth I attained heaven, I prefer to be free in the immensity. Am I right?

A strange woman, who feels in herself such a force that links her to something beyond and sets her apart from the world! The future author Catherine Pozzi (who studied under Marie on a weekly basis as an adolescent, and who continued to work with her later in life, as well) penned a portrait of Marie in 1914 which is surprisingly predictive of so much of what she became half a century later:

> No human person is as fascinating. I believe the dominant sentiment that emanates from her is greatness, something that the Prophets undoubtedly had. For they, from their narrow present, saw the house of centuries ripen. Like them, she feels and contemplates within her the figure of the harvests of life. But she outdoes them since she scatters the seeds to the wind with her curious little steely hands. Will they grow like the mustard grains? She thinks so, and that explains why the true must appear immortal to the soul that has tasted it well. Alas! It has left in mine only the despair of too beautiful a gift to be accepted by the world.

Sometime after her marriage, Marie entered a mystical period where passion, love, faith, and desire for the absolute clashed violently within her heart that was in pursuit of the divine. She immersed herself in moral, religious and human as well as scientific problems. She read and worked tremendously to fill the gaps in her education. As usual, she undertook her self-education with great ardor and drive.

"I always feel the enormous weight of things I do not know," she wrote, "I would like to turn days into years, and work all the time. Time passes, and there seems to be no end to work."

In the meanwhile, she spent her boundless energy publicizing controversial musical works like Berlioz's *Benvenuto Cellini*, an epic historical comedy. This masterpiece with its inventive and engaging music celebrates the evolution of an artisan into an artist. When first performed, around 1832, it was greeted with lusty *boo*'s by the public. In fact, Berlioz, the musical figure of great daring and grand ideas, had passed away in 1869, no longer believing in God, or in himself, or in anyone, and abandoned by everyone. His compositions, each of them a masterpiece, were loose in form and marked by a highly emotional personal style. They are self-projected at a scale larger than life, and proclaim the true spirit of Romanticism in its depth. This composer of the unbounded was ill-appreciated, especially in his home country. Only exceptional personalities could sense his genius. The generous Liszt had met him in his youth in 1830 at the first performance of the *Symphonie Fantastique*. It was a revelation to him; he applauded rapturously, and on the spot invited Berlioz to his home.

"Liszt, the famous pianist, took me by force, so to speak, to dinner at his place, overwhelming me with all that is energetic in enthusiasm," wrote Berlioz to his father. Liszt, the tenderhearted gypsy, and Berlioz, the tortured soul, met each other in the mysterious realms where artists are brothers. From the very start the Hungarian recognized the genius of the young Frenchman, and hailed the awe-inspiring *"Symphonie Fantastique"* as the most perfect musical expression of the Romantic genius. A solid friendship bound the two men, though Berlioz, embittered at the end of his life, struck some false notes. These did not prevent Liszt from having his friend's works performed at Weimar.

Marie Jaëll's Romantic heart could not but be enthused for the music of this great and unique musician. She defended his restless and elemental music with passion, and played them with such conviction and enthusiasm "that she ended by persuading you," a critic noted.

It was at this time that she decided to take her first lessons in composition with César Franc and Camille Saint-Saëns.

Saint Saëns is one of the big names of French music of the latter half of the century. In 1871, backed by the leading musicians of his time, he founded the "Société Nationale de Musique, Ars Gallica" to defend and French music which was in full bloom, personified by Indy, Duparc, Fauré, Gounod... Quite a few young composers owed their careers to him. He knew how to spot new talents. With close attention he followed Marie's first steps in composition.

Thus, she was ready to take the step that let her enter the world of composers. She sent her first pieces, completed in 1871, to her steadfast and considerate friend Liszt, who wrote to her:

I have read with passionate attention your meditations, impromptus, little pieces, and the big sonata; they abound in novelties and boldness, but perhaps, should you bend your great and dazzling talent not to concessions but to certain adjustments that are difficult to fix. We will speak about them amicably.

In 1878, she composed a musical drama called *Runéa*. Only a few isolated pages of it survive. She also wrote *Ossiane*, a romantic opera. A part of it was performed at Erard's, though most of Marie's creations were played at Pleyel's. Again, only bits of it have come down to us. Liszt played a behind-the-scene role to promote her compositions.

After the performance of a part of *Ossiane*, one critic wrote a penetrating review that highlighted the virile character of the her work.

Marie Jaëll, who, as a virtuoso, has won all the laurels an artist can obtain, today aspires to the title of composer; this title has been awarded to many others who do not deserve it. She is a woman, it is true; but that fact is not perceived in her music. What rapture, what boldness, what virility!

Oh! Her enterprise, we must admit, is one of the most reckless since it makes the heroine Ossiane attain nothing less than the divine pinnacle inhabited by the god of harmony: it is not by singing the barcarolle that a mortal can hope to face the eternal flames that surround him.

I will not wait to know the work in full to affirm the presence of an exceptional musical talent, amazing gifts and qualities of the highest order in the author of Ossiane. No woman has ever shown such power, such energy, such willpower.

Her works are astonishing. They reveal her powerful nature. People often speak of her as a volcano. "A man's name on your music," Liszt told her, "and it will be on every piano."

Camille Saint-Saëns compared his pupil's first attempts to the irruption of a devastating torrent. In the meantime, her works were well received by critics.

When she interpreted her *Concerto for Piano in D minor* with the Cologne orchestra at Châtelet, a music critic reported, "The work and its virtuoso author received the best ovation."

Her works were played in the greatest Parisian halls.

Filling the Erard hall [one reads in the *Music Gazette* of Paris], has become the privilege of truly great concerts; it was so with that of Mr. and Mrs. Jaëll ... But a greater part of the interest of this concert was attached to Mme Marie Jaëll's second début as a composer. Everyone remembers her first, last year, with a piano quartet; this time Mme Marie Jaëll presented the public with waltzes for four hands. It is highly remarkable, and far superior to what could normally be expected from a woman...

Liszt took upon himself the task of editing her waltzes. He even played them with Saint-Saëns at Bayreuth.

Marie composed prolifically for the piano as well as for other instruments, and songs. Her "*Fantasy for Violin*" was played at the Société Nationale under the direction of Vincent d'Indy at Antwerp. Her *Sur la tombe d'un enfant* for choir and orchestra, composed after the death of a child of Saint-Saëns', was played in many places. All her pieces were played in several countries and especially in Germany.

In the meantime a great concern came to torment and affect Marie's life. Her husband's health began to decline. As the years passed, his diabetes got worse. The summer of 1879 took the couple to Prague for a concert tour. It was to be Alfred's last journey abroad. Too exhausted, he was sometimes forced to interrupt his concert in the middle...

"Alas, Alfred is so unwell," she wrote, "that I really fear he will not recover."

"I must go on with courage. Alfred is seriously ill. He himself realizes that there is no longer any hope; but everything is difficult in this world: to die and to live both are so, sometimes, and it is with fear that I look at myself."

Alfred passed away on February 27, 1882, leaving Marie, whom he had dragged across Europe in a whirlwind of tours, alone at the age 35.

Liszt learnt the news when he was in Budapest. He immediately sent these words to Marie:

> Dear Admirable,
> Life and death, the same mystery! Let us raise our hearts through faith and hope; that they purify, sustain, console, idealize our Love and make it worthy of heavenly origin and end.
> Yours cordially devoted
> F. Liszt

Marie felt the loss of Alfred deeply. Her diary presents a bleak picture of this period of her life: "I must admit it was night, and without illusions, plunged into darkness, and gazing into nothingness."

She was all the more alone as she had lost her mother a short time before Alfred's death. Her mother's passing left an immense emptiness; she had taken such an active part in Marie's life of music with understanding, solicitude and love. In this period Marie returned often to her Alsace, where she felt at home. Her father even had a little wooden cottage built for her, behind their home, to house a piano, a table and some chairs.

> Here in Steinseltz, I am in ecstasy, today my stay here is an enchantment. I am grateful to this stimulating spell of time that gives me an occasion to think and discover nature's life forces.

There, in the lengthening shadows of tall, silent trees, Marie worked frantically. She took delight in composing, writing, and perfecting her piano playing. "I am in the garden," she exclaims, "I feel I am a blade of grass, a bird, a pine-tree, a flower, a plum-tree, a chestnut-tree, I am the blue sky...." Her homeland would always be a source of peace for her, and a sense of being rooted. Its intense and profound nature filled her, inspired her, gave her once again the sense of harmony "which we unconsciously carry in us," and which she often felt that she had lost.

>...We must seek harmony, not happiness [she writes]; happiness comes from outside, harmony comes from within; it is natural, happiness is feigned, harmony dwells in us, happiness flees. Through harmony we are born aloft to universal truth, through happiness we are bound to earthly truth.
>...Harmony is above destiny, above life's discords; it can also reside in sadness. Beethoven's marvelous adagios are a proof of it. Who is not happy to listen to them though they are sad? Grief, sadness ought not be considered as provoking necessarily discordances in us.
>...It is relatively easy to conceive harmony in art, but how much our subjective underestimation makes the art of life difficult!

In spite of her grief, Marie always went forward, with an élan and sense of independence that seemed to drive her. She threw herself into composition. Saint-Saëns followed his pupil's progress with interest; yet relations between the two were sometimes strained. Saint-Saëns himself did not have a gentle character, far from it; he was over-sensitive and easily annoyed; his remarks could be scathing. Once he lamented, "I am too nervous today. I did not sleep during the night. I will be odious and insufferable."

Their deep and difficult friendship was interrupted by storms, estrangements, break-ups and reconciliation. "I have been absurd and guilty, excuse me," pleaded Saint-Saëns after a fiery exchange. But they always had a mutual respect and they recognized each other's talents. He dedicated to her his first concerto and his étude in waltz form.

It must be noted that Marie's nature was also unyielding. She too was quick-tempered and had her own mind. Liszt, a patient man, attempted a reconciliation, but it does not last long.

In 1887, Camille Saint-Saëns, seconded by Fauré, proposed Marie's candidature to the "Société des Compositeurs de Musique." She received her letters of admission in October.

Madame, I have the honor to inform you that at your request and at the suggestion of Mr Saint-Saëns and Mr. Fauré, our Committee at its meeting of October 31 1887 has pronounced your admission as an active member of the *Société des Compositeurs de Musique*.
Please accept, Madame, the expression of our most devoted sentiments...

Marie thus became one of the very first women to enter officially this Society.

Composition seemed to come easily to her; yet the pages of her diary reveal nagging doubts:

In two months, so many works have been produced... This growing productive capacity does not give me peace, and yet I consider all that I write just a preliminary stage for a distant goal.
...I am making progress, though,... Alas, what torments me is how to discern if what I write belongs to me or is taken from others...

Marie Jaëll composed in almost all musical genres. More than 80 of her compositions were published during her lifetime. They are remarkable and they show the difficulties French music had in freeing itself from German models. They mark the transition from the great German Romantic music of the early nineteenth century to the French music of late nineteenth century of Fauré, Gounod, Debussy and Ravel.

LISZT'S SCHOOL

After 1883, Marie took up the habit of sojourning at Weimar in the company of her friend Liszt. Wagner, his son-in-law, had just passed away, felled by a heart attack some months after the first performance of *Parsifal*. This work, deemed Wagner's spiritual and musical testament, is a work of farewell to the world and to life. Liszt would say that it was "more than a masterpiece, it is a revelation in musical drama." He was present at the first representation, surrounded by Chausson, Vincent d'Indy, Saint-Saëns, all of whom were aware of taking part in one of the great events of the century. Lou Salomé, who was also there, moved to the depths of her heart, knelt before Wagner to kiss his hands. "The eternal principle of life is in this work," Marie would say, after having listened to *Parsifal* at Bayreuth.

Wagner's death does not seem to have affected Liszt very much. He wrote, "Dying seems simpler to me than living...." Without any apparent emotion, he whispered, "Him today, me tomorrow..."

He was no longer the flamboyant and fiery virtuoso of the beginning of the century. Little by little his life tended towards renunciation. His separation from Marie d'Agoult had taken place long ago. They had three children: Blandine, Cosima — who had become Wagner's wife, and Daniel. Liszt, having borne the grief of losing Blandine and Daniel at an early age, had only Cosima left to him.

He spent much of his best time at Weimar, where he was still the Master of the Chapel. But he continued to cover Europe, mainly between France and Hungary.

Notorious in his youth for his piano showmanship and virtuosity, he mellowed with advancing age; but the magic of his fingers at the piano stayed undimmed. Ever since he arrived at the Weimar court, he was oblivious of his past successes. He kept busy with works of high composition, and he worked for a renewal of art. His dynamism was upsetting to his contemporaries who saw, in his exploration of a new world, the desire to break with traditions. From the very beginning the Weimar School, as it came to be called, was seen as being revolutionary, in opposition to the Dresden school personified by Schumann and Brahms.

Ever since Liszt had taken charge of the music programs of Weimar, his avant-garde school (one of whose members was Wagner) had made a clean break with the conventions of the classical epoch of Romanticism. Many visitors came to knock at his door, to take courses or simply out of curiosity, to get a glimpse of the great man.

Thus he met Alexander Borodin, who came straight from Russia to make his acquaintance. Not well understood in his own country, he had suffered a setback with his symphony in E-minor. Liszt, ever generous and fair, gave him confidence and encouraged him: "Good music at first meets with nothing but indifference or hostility." And he added, "You have an original talent. Don't listen to anyone, and do your work your own way."

Borodin visited him a second time. Through him, Liszt took interest in the New Russia represented by Balakirev, Moussorgsky, Tchaikovsky and others. He also had the pleasure of welcoming his dear friends like Camille Saint-Saëns, who brought the young Gabriel Fauré, still unsure and hesitant before the great Liszt, who was a living legend. Fauré already foreshadowed the impressionist music of the end of the nineteenth century. He stood for the new world of sound that was being born, and was a prophet of the coming century. People assured him that "his music would be the harmonic language of the future."

In a surprising way, Liszt's new compositions also prefigured the music to come. The man had changed. He gradually turned his back on the world's clamors. He abandoned the virtuoso arabesques to make room for silence, and the musical works of his old age plunge us into great emotion. They reflect his withdrawal into solitude. In them we also discover one of the essential sources of modern music. He looked at the world through a painter's senses as much as a musician's. In his last pieces, like *"Gray Clouds,"* his music verges on silence, that silence that, in the words of the mystic Christian poet St. Jean de La Croix, helps us "divine the soul's song."

During one of his trips to Italy, Liszt composed magnificent pieces for the piano at the Villa d'Este: *The Cypresses of Villa d'Este* and *Fountains of the Villa d'Este*. They already were paving the way for musicians like Ravel and Debussy.

His pages seem to be the fruit of his reflection during the nostalgic moments of the evening of his life. Looking back at his past, he saw once more the beloved faces, weeping, dreaming, regretting, and always inventing love. It is a music permeated by reflections, perfumes, fluid melodies gushing forth from water to drop like gold or silver dust, cherishing the dreams of a man in wonder, but also troubled by the flight of time.

After hearing Liszt play, a British visitor who was passing through recounted that, "With his right hand he began to play a rhythmic motif that sounded like the peal of evening bells. He seemed to be lost in a dream... Suddenly, from under the left hand burst forth the sound of Angelus, or rather, what a rambler in the countryside might have heard while passing by the ruins of a cloister as the ghosts of monks chanted their prayers at nightfall."

Liszt was in the final period of his life. During his declining years, Marie Jaëll saw him often; and she decided to spend some months with him in 1883. "Don't go near Liszt," one of her friends advised her, "he is capable of drying up the buoyant sap of your individuality. He may try to graft a shoot of his own on the sturdy stem of your thought."

But Marie let her instincts guide her. She knew that no influence, however mighty, could lead her astray. She countered by saying, "I could not find a friend, protector and master better than him."

She left for Weimar in April, and she stayed for more than six months in Liszt's company at Hofgaertnerai, where he held court. She took an active part in the musical life that gravitated around him. She worked with him, and followed his lessons. At times she worked as his secretary. Occasionally, she proofread for him, since his eyesight had begun to fail.

The years at Weimar were the last Liszt spent with his numerous pupils and friends. Marie met and mixed with most of them: Jules Zaremski, the Polish virtuoso who died young while playing Chopin's funeral march, the Russian Siloti, Felix Weingartner, prestigious composer and chef d'orchestre, and Albeniz, who arrived there at the age of eighteen to perfect his tantalizing virtuosity with Liszt.

Eugene d'Albert, the supremely talented young Scottish pianist, was also present. Of fragile health, he fell seriously ill. Liszt, fearing the worst, asked Marie to watch over his prestigious student. She knew that Eugene was alone in the world, and she looked after him with devotion. Her diary bears witness to the bonds of deep friendship between them.

The days at Weimar were devoted to course work, concerts and public events. The intrigues spinning around the exhausted Liszt and the life at Weimar were at times hard for Marie, coming from such a simple background. Yet she stayed on, for her affection for the Master was boundless, and she always had the feeling that she was learning more while observing him. The evolution and perfection of her art were her intense and constant concern. Her diary speaks of this thirst for work:

> Today, I have a right to complain. I wasted my day. What an abominable thing! Nothing is comparable to the happiness of being able to work.
> I am singularly silent, I have work fever, and it must be gratified. I love my art with an extraordinary passion; how wonderful to live with this flame. What is curious is that it seems to grow all the time, its light inundates me more and more, I see it becoming bigger like the rising sun. What brightness!

The experience at Weimar was a plus and a minus for Marie. On the one hand, it was a sort of school for her. On the other hand, it was a den of intrigues.

She observed, listened, exchanged ideas on music and literature as the opportunities presented themselves; and she gave concerts with Liszt. With her generous and great-hearted nature, she took interest in everything that touched the human being.

> We must live in order to know others. We must see them, to draw from them as much as we can all that is beautiful in them, get shaped in contact with them, form an opinion, look for the good, appreciate it, be watchful with generous eyes that shrink at nothing. How to attain such an attitude? Know truly to love, and you will find.

It was not easy to work in Weimar. There were too many people, too many conventions, too many intrigues.

> If I have to spend a great many days like this one, in Weimar, I cannot not hold out for long.
> It is true I must find my bearings; I cannot live like this. I must have my great inner heaven, the gleam that shines at the bottom of my soul, and which dominates so well the darkness that is outside. This gleam is my life, it must come back to me; where has it gone? I have not felt it for a few days, it is as if I am no longer myself.
> I feel like I am smeared with all sorts of colors. I have to wash myself to recover the skin to which I am attached. I cannot carry on like this. I need my four walls and wide paths towards heaven, I look then at high above and I see something that corresponds to it.
> To stay here at Weimar, what strength, what perseverance I need!
> The love of progress pushed to the limit.... Yes, in spite of everything, I stay on. For, I am not in a position to stand by myself. I must still draw from quite a few sources, learn quite a few things, and find quite a few truths. That is why I am here, for my affection for Liszt would be quite unable to keep me for long. For that, I need my life's dominant willpower that sums up almost all my existence in one and the same action...'
> I am sea-sick. I may leave Weimar any day.

In fact, Marie did leave Weimar soon after that note, but returned the following year. This second stay definitely went off better.

> This year, life at Weimar is almost ideal for me. I will take advantage of it artistically and intellectually in the broadest sense of the word.

In 1885, for the third and last time Marie returned to Weimar to be with Liszt. She did not write much during this last sojourn. As she was leaving for Paris, he entrusted a part of his personal diary to her. But an unbelievable thing happened. Marie left it in the train! She could never be consoled for her incredible carelessness. Fortunately, the generous-hearted Liszt pardoned her.

In the meanwhile, he undertook one last tour of Europe in remembrance of all the concerts he had given in the different capitals since his youth: Venice, Budapest, London and Paris, where his "Gran Mass" (Missa Solennis) was to be played.

He dreaded, a little, the stopover in the French capital, for he remembered the failure of its first performance in 1866 which had been such a painful setback for him. At that time people reproached him for his friendship for Wagner, the avant-garde genius musician. "In contemporary art at this time," he wrote, "there is a name that will be more and more glorious: Richard Wagner. His genius has been a torch for me.

But it was hard for the new music to find a place in the public's heart. The first performance of the Gran Mass at Saint Eustache in 1866 met the same fate as the Tannhaüser five years earlier. Even the opening of Lohengrin a week earlier was given only a lukewarm reception.

Marie d'Agoult, not really recovered from her separation from Liszt, set to work against him and raised the hackles of the musical press. At her urging, they went attacked The Gran Mass and its author.

It is thus that Liszt was called names like "the henchman of Wagnerism." One caustic critic wrote, "in short, this mass is nothing but a somber symphony as the musicians of the future will hear it. In search of scientific depth without concerning about melody, they will run the risk of praising it for the dryness of its form..."

Berlioz himself, embittered and exhausted by his failures, despite his close friendship with Liszt (to whom he had dedicated his Damnation of Faust) declared to one of his friends: "Yesterday there was a performance of Liszt's Mass. There was a huge crowd. But alas, what a denial of art!" A little later, he had the following text printed:

> Abbé Liszt's Mass, as a whole and in details, is so upsetting to the notions a long practice has instilled in my mind on melody,

harmony, modulation and rhythm, manner and form, manner of presenting, of treating, developing a motif tonality, concordance between music and word etc. that I can only own my defect of perception, declare my incompetence and decline to give my opinion. I have religiously listened to Abbé Liszt's Mass at the general rehearsal and execution. God knows what I have suffered, and what I still suffer in not being able to admire this work of a great pianist, of a genius pianist whose talent sent me into ecstasies so many times, and whose person will be always dear to me.

In sum, it was a quarrel between the "Old" and the "Modern" taking place through two friends. The future is often right, and Liszt had every reason to be happy to be among the Moderns.

Concerning the performance, Liszt himself wrote:

> One third of the hall applauded, and a certain number of people even applauded warmly. A group of around fifteen formed a cabal, some individuals imprudently called for a *bis*. People were saying here and there that it is a great work, we must hear it again.

So Liszt was of two minds concerning his return to Paris. His Mass was to be performed at the Church Saint Eustace, just like the first time twenty years earlier. He wrote to Marie Jaëll:

> Admirable Ossiana (this is what he called her, alluding to her symphonic poem *Ossiane*),
> I hesitate to come back to Paris. The unhappy experience of the *Gran Mass* at Saint Eustace still weighs on me — not without reason, though without ill will. It's best for me to continue my work, for better or worse, and look for no other pleasure, — that is enough for me. Presenting myself either as a young composer for the audience to boo, or as an old *emeritus* pianist for the audience to complain about ("He's not what he used to be"), is scarcely appealing; and I do not think that any better role than these two is reserved for me. Either way, my reputation would not be enhanced.

Finally, he decided to visit Paris in March 1886 and attend the audition of his work conducted by Colonne. Jean Chantavoinne gives a glowing description of the event.

The impression was awe-inspiring and profound, heightened by the appearance of the white-haired old man who bent his superb head to join a silent prayer to the accents of the music. It was a success!

The following day the Parisian musical world met at Erard's place to listen and honor the great man for one last time. He also played for some friends, at Marie Jaëll's salon. He wrote to her:

Listen, dear Ossiana, let's get together, and let's give a concert — Jaëll-Liszt — at your place for a select gathering. It would be great. Invite our friend Saint-Saëns and some others of your choice. No fireworks, nor tra la la — only intimate music.
Admiration and affection.
F. Liszt.

After the performance, Liszt left Paris, and Marie never saw him again.

"I am extremely fatigued with life... and I am good for nothing any more," he confessed in May. On July 31 of the same year, he breathed his last.

He penned his own epitaph: "O my God! You have given me what could be given to anyone here below: everything, everything! Let me fall asleep, alone and forgotten."

After having been a legendary pianist, genius transcriber and an improviser ahead of his times, this generous musician, gypsy and Franciscan, terribly human and so close to God, managed to leave his imprint in the infinite spaces of the future. As he had once asked, "Is our life anything else but a series of preludes to that unknown song, whose first and solemn note is intoned by death?"

Marie Jaëll was deeply affected by Liszt's death. The way this extraordinary pianist played had been a deep revelation to her. The lasting bonds of friendship that linked them as accomplices in art and vision of man and God were unique.

The loss of such a close friend marked a decisive turning point in her life. From then on she abandoned herself entirely to the analysis of musical touch. "It is not what I am accomplishing that absorbs my passion," she would write later, "it is the feeling that I have discovered Liszt's spirit in me, and that it could be transmitted to future generations. What a holy joy to be able to hope that it may be so."

2. The Piano Saga

The Piano, The Prince of Instruments

During his lifetime Liszt was hailed as "the king of pianists." There is no doubt that his life and work are central to an understanding of piano music. At the time of his death, the piano reigned supreme among musical instruments, and had reached its present day technical perfection. Three distinct periods punctuate its ascent to pre-eminence: the years of gestation, 1700-1770; of decision, 1770-1850; and of glory, 1850-1970. Its invention was driven by a search for crystal-pure sounds highlighting harmony in order to give vent to personal sentiments in the social context of triumphant individualism. Groping their way through trial and error, musicians at first grafted simple improvements onto existing instruments. At a critical juncture, genius composers, virtuoso performers and master craftsmen all joined hands to fashion "the prince of instruments."

The piano did not just "happen." It was consciously and painstakingly created to meet deeply felt social and individual needs. To get a glimpse of the forces that were at work, that coalesced in leading to its invention, we have to delve deeply into the wellsprings of European music. Truly, the best theory of piano is its history. It alone can explain why the piano, in contrast to other musical instruments, shot up so swiftly from infancy to maturity.

Music is sound, organized according to a pattern. It is not noise whose defining feature is irregularity of vibrations hitting the eardrum. Music, by contrast, is characterized by the periodicity of notes and the presence of sustained tones. The continuously changing relationships among its components are structured around three fundamentals: harmony, rhythm and melody. A note, with an expressive pointer attached to it, expresses harmony. Melody conveys the thought content underlying a piece of music. Rhythm, the pulse and symbol of music's vitality, is the engine that powers it forward.

Unfairly, music is sometimes called "heightened speech." In a spoken phrase like, "I love you passionately," melody would correspond to "I love you" and harmony to "passionately." Stress or accent on words endows it with rhythm: "I *love* you" or "I love *you.*"

Of the three, rhythm is the universal, and in many musical idioms, the primary constituent. It reflects the changes of flow of sounds in time. It is omnipresent in nature to express life, movement and regularity. There is also a certain rhythm in our speech and our bodily movements. Unfortunately, its precise role in the evolution of man-made music is yet to be made clear. In any case, without it, harmony and melody would be paralyzed. By its nature it provides a background. In vocal music, it is the prisoner of the flow of words. Keyboard music frees it from such constraints.

Pitch is the height of a tone. It defines the quality of sound as a function of its fundamental frequency. A single tone, depending on its volume and duration, can be deeply stirring. A chord is the simultaneous combination of three to five tones, called triads. It forms the building block of harmony and melody.

Harmony, the vertical dimension of music, is the deliberate and conscious combination of notes of identifiable pitch. Its implications are always latent in every sequence of notes. It came to the forefront only late development in the history of music. It then became a powerful weapon to convey emotion in the particular. Its centrality in music since the eighteenth century is a distinguishing feature of Western culture.

Melody is the horizontal dimension of music. In consciously created sounds, it involves a change of pitch and tone, and is embedded in a series of chords. It always comes in waves, in the form of jumps along tones. It represents the sense of musical flow across phrases. Its components are fragments of musical scale, with harmonic pointers that stimulate when they rise and bring a sense of release when they fall. It is always interpreted both at the source and the destination.

While rhythm can live on its own, melody and harmony are structurally interdependent. Since both of them share an interval, an inbuilt tension exists between them. Analyzing a melody is like slicing a complex harmonic sound into its overtones and laying them out in a particular order. The Romantics first explored the emotional potential of the harmony of a single pitch before endowing melodic phrases or a sequence of harmonies with expressive power.

For a long time, Western music gave primacy to melody over harmony. It evolved horizontally by emphasizing melodic lines. It was vocal, without supporting instruments. Church hymns were no more than an unaccompanied melody moving through a relatively small range of tones. The Gregorian chant was conceived as pure melody; it was never intended to have any harmonic support. Organ music followed the same path, enriched by two or four parallel strands. "The ear was directed to follow the movement of two three or four voices from chord to chord without any regard for the meaning of individual chords."[45] Musical notation gave clusters of tones to indicate the rhythmic pattern but not the value of each tone. The rhythm was continually bent to accommodate the words.

Church music was almost entirely congregational. Religious composers were expected to efface, if not suppress, their personality in the music they created. Innovation took the form of counterpoint.

---

45. Schenker Harmony, p.154

Two or more melodic lines would pursue independent courses, each having a more or less equal claim to listeners' attention. Their interplay and interdependence were the bases of the pleasure that such music gave.

During the twelfth century instrumental music made its entrance. Crusaders returning from the Middle East brought a large variety of music instruments. As early as 1323, Jean du Muris in his *Ars Speculativa* mentions several keyboard instruments that are clear precursors of the clavichord and harpsichord. During Medieval and Renaissance times, vocal music was regarded as an activity of the mind, and instrument players were relegated to the rank of technicians.[46] In its supporting role, instrumental music imitated vocal technique.

Both vocal and instrumental music marched forward, enriching each other through mutual feedback. Segments of Gregorian chant, shorn of their religious significance but maintaining their emphasis on melody, made their way into popular song. Pure instrumental music emerged during the thirteenth century, for dancing purposes. Non-religious tunes then began to filter into Church music. In 1234, the Pope outlawed the mingling of voices, unnatural rhythms, and indecently fast speeds for religious purposes. His decree froze ecclesiastical music at the plainsong level. Progress in the world of music then took a secular turn and it soon enjoyed the backing of aristocratic patrons. The new music soon reflected French, German, Italian and English nationalist temperaments. Musical notation also underwent changes and began to indicate the duration of individual notes, while emphasizing their context.

The "Autumn of the Middle Ages" inaugurated an intellectual revolution. It brought individualism to the forefront. It proposed an optimistic vision of man. The new trend was first manifest in visual arts like painting. Then, "the idea of music as a vehicle of ideas, composed with the purpose of penetrating the mind of man and

---

46. Koningberger, D., *Renaissance Man and Creative Thinking*, Harvester Press 1979 p.177

producing the renowned effects, took root."[47] Composers began expressing personal emotions. Their energies found outlets in opera and instrumental music.

To give voice to human feelings in opera, the musicians preferred the symbolic figures of classical mythology to biblical persons. But their idealized expression of sentiments was not that different from the detached Church music. Within the opera, the solo singer, with his music of surprising intensity, became the focus of emotions. At the same time, instrumental music ceased to be subservient to words and to the steps of dancers.

Gradually instrumental music asserted its independence. It found inspiration in repetitive rhythms rooted in bodily movements. In the atmosphere of newfound freedom, solo keyboard performers thrived. Both opera and keyboard instruments, as they interacted, widened the emotional range of music. Italy, land of sun and open spaces, excelled in opera, and in Northern Europe, continent of cold winters and homebound culture, keyboard instruments prevailed. Italy also revolutionized violin music. Paganini (1782-1840) dazzled the world of music by his virtuoso techniques for violin that Liszt later transferred to the piano.

By 1740, Italy stood supreme as the land of opera. The great composers like Rossini, Donizetti and Bellini thought primarily in melodic terms. The full opera, where the emphasis is concentrated on voice (called "the natural instrument") provided them with a rich palette of sound-color. They also gave the solo singer an opportunity to express himself. But the rhythmic and harmonic support they gave to the vocal line tended to be faint, so the solo singer's expressive phrases were accompanied by relatively static harmonies. These were selected with great subtlety to bring out the emotional content of the words.

The keyboard instruments, capable of providing both harmony and melody, made the first substantial contribution to soloists. The English produced music that was genuinely instrumental — it was

47. *Ibidem*

not a vocal concept transferred to the keyboard.[48] Thus they not only invented the sounds themselves but also brought into being the resources needed to create them.

Between 1730 and 1770, the economies of Western Europe turned a corner and shortly exploded into the Industrial Revolution. During the same decades a profound and subtle qualitative change overtook European music. "People began to compose music in new ways, listen to it in new ways and think about it in new ways.[49] The need to convey emotion in personal terms brought attention to harmony as a positive force. Composers tried to transfer their success with the opera to keyboard instruments. For example, Haendel treated the voice more as an instrument than as a bearer of verbal messages. From Haydn onwards, orchestral sound, marked by wonderful outbursts, echoed in all instrumental music.

Thus musicians, in search of unalloyed sounds, moved away from the heavy ornamental Baroque style and embraced a clean, uncluttered style. The counterpoint, till then on the ascendant, yielded its place to a clear homophonic texture. The vertical chord dimension became dominant. In the new set-up, the role of melody and rhythm had to be re-invented.

The new orientation made functional harmony a focal point of music. Following the new style, musicians were forced to mold musical phrases by separating melody from accompaniment. As a result, they struggled to find or adapt instruments that could produce nuances and dynamic variations. Clavichords and harpsichords, instruments then in vogue, were wanting in such qualities.

The clavichord was a simple but subtle stringed-key instrument. Its origins can be traced to the Middle Ages. It had a rectangular keyboard and two strings for each note, hence the term bi-chord. Depressing a key caused a thin brass blade, called a "tangent," to move up and strike the string. The player's fingers

---

48. Hopkins, A.

49. *Oxford Dictionary of Music*, p. 620

could maintain a constant control over the strings so that he directly mastered the volume and color of the tone. He could also obtain sensitive gradations of tone, and even a *vibrato*. Thus the directness of touch was responsible for both dynamics and expressiveness.

But the player would knock the clavichord out of tune if he tried for loud sonority. This was its greatest shortcoming, and made it unsuitable for public concerts. It was an instrument for meditation, intimacy and private amusement. It was most popular in German-speaking countries, where many of the patrons of music were princes and ecclesiastics.

The harpsichord, on the other hand, was loud enough, and was the most brilliant of all instruments of the time. It consisted of tuned strings held taut in a wooden case. They were plucked by a small plectrum, originally made of quill. A player obtained sound variety not through finger pressure but more subtly, by phrasing and articulation. Thus, the "terraced dynamic" it offered was produced mechanically rather than through immediate control by the player's fingers.

Harpsichords appeared towards the beginning of the sixteenth century. They were essentially of two types. Those in Italy were lightly constructed and encased in wood. They had an immediate, and even percussive tone, and answered well the needs of seventeenth-century Italian music. North European harpsichords were solidly built. They could give a powerful tone, with a reedy treble and a sonorous bass. Two or three sets of strings per key, tuned either to the same pitch or with one set sounding an octave higher, were used for contrast of tone and coupling in order to obtain a fuller sound. As time went on, the manufacturers increased the compass in both treble and bass.

Due to its loudness, it was the ideal keyboard instrument for public performances. Almost until the end of the eighteenth century, it was the most popular of all keyboard instruments. It occupied a special place in French court-centered music.

It also had several pitfalls. Even the best harpsichord needed constant care, re-quilling and re-voicing. Above all, it could not yield subtle gradations of volume: the harpsichord is a plucked instrument, so there is no possibility of modulating the sound's volume the way one can do, in the case of the piano, by varying one's touch. In the piano, the multiple strings for the same note are linked to the soundboard differently; the strings are not tuned identically.

Musicians tried to conceal the intrinsic shortcomings of their instruments by their artistry and by appealing to the sensitive response of listeners. Keyboard players were always enjoined to "sing." This, however, was almost impossible since in all keyboard string instruments, each note fades as soon as it begins to sound. Some performers tried to give the harpsichord a *crescendo* and a *diminuendo* by rapidly changing the register of keys.

Johann Sebastian Bach, a central figure of European music, even wrote a manual for keyboard instrumentalists. He felt that tones, if they were not detached from each other, would "sing." Unfortunately, the excessive use of rapid notes made it quite difficult to give a "singing" performance of an *adagio* without creating too much empty space or running the risk of self-caricature; he was impelled to imagine the construction of better instruments.

The search for instruments that emphasized harmony went on all over Western Europe. Then certain musicians hit on an idea for modifying their keyboard instruments in a promising way. Cristofori (1655-1730), in Florence, experimented with hammer mechanics at the turn of the seventeenth century. By 1708 he had invented and perfected the hammer action and replaced harpsichord's plectra by hammers.

Other musicians immediately began to talk up the bold invention. And, they soon realized that the new instrument called for a different "touch," since the nature of the sound produced was a function of the force with which the performer struck the keys. Above all, they were enthralled that they could play it not only *piano* and *forte* but also impart to it a gradation and diversity of power. In 1732, the composer Giustini published twelve sonatas for Cristofori's instrument, indicating *piano et forte* — guides to the performer — "soft" and "loud." The new instrument came to be called pianoforte, and then just piano.

The dynamics that spurred musicians was the obsession with clarity of sound. Cristofori designed a mechanism called "escapement" to prevent the hammer from bouncing back after striking, and hitting the string a second time. Now, the hammer "escapes" the string after striking it, and the string vibrates freely, producing a set of confused sounds. For that reason each note, with the general exception of the last twenty high notes, was given a felt-covered wooden piece called the damper, which in its normal position reposed upon the string and prevented it from vibrating after neighboring strings were struck. As a key is struck, the metal stem fixed on the individual mechanism of the hammer lets the damper climb lightly at the moment the hammer strikes. When the hammer withdraws, the damper falls back on the string, and extinguishes the tone. Consequently the resulting sounds remained distinct or are fused harmoniously. Cristofori's inventions assured the proper functioning of repeated tones.

Traditional histories of the piano narrate that Cristofori's innovation did not find favor in his hometown where orchestra rather than instrumental music was the order of the day. In fact, the first great advocate of the piano was Scarlatti (1685-1757). Throughout his career, he played the piano and composed for it. Thanks to him, it became popular in Southern Europe during the first half of the eighteenth century.[50]

As news of Cristofori's invention spread through Northern Europe, enthusiasm grew. His instrument was adopted in Venice and a sketch of its action was published there in 1711. A book describing the innovation appeared in German in 1725. The new technology soon spread through printed and verbal accounts and spontaneous experimentation. The traditional organ makers now turned to the manufacture of the new instrument. In 1725, G.

50. Sutherland D., "Dominico Scarlatti and the Florentine Piano," *Early Music*, May 1995 :243-256.

Silbermann in Freiburg constructed similar instruments. J.S. Bach tested some of them. He found their action heavy and their treble register weak, so he remained faithful to the clavichord and harpsichord. He did find a later model to his liking, however, and the two fugues in his *Musical Offering* were probably written in the knowledge that they would be played on the piano.[51]

The piano then inched forward between the years 1760-80. Two models, distinct in character and design, came to life, and quite different music was written for them. The Viennese model, built by J.A. Stein (1728-92) around 1770, grafted the new technology onto the clavichord. It was a lightly built bi-chord instrument with a thin, flat soundboard and tiny leather-covered hammers. Its beautiful but thin tone suggested a louder clavichord. Its touch was shallow and required less force, so it was simpler and more direct. It called for light action and gave a clear and intimate sound. It could also sing and create flowing melodic lines. Its bass was rich but not overpowering, as in a harpsichord.

England was home to the other model. John Broadwood, a Scottish carpenter, worked with Schudi, a Swiss harpsichord maker in London. An apprentice of Silbermann, J. C. Zumpe, moved to London in 1760. After working with Schudi, he became a successful manufacturer of square pianos, shaped like a clavichord. Broadwood, Shudi's son-in-law, reconstructed Zumpe's design. He straightened the keys, improved the dampers and replaced Zumpe's hand stops by "loud" and "soft" pedals. After patenting his improvements he turned to the design of grand pianos that came to be named after him. The piano scored its first wave of success in 1768 in England, and London became the center of innovation in piano making. It brought manufacturers, composers and pianists together so that their individual techniques could be streamlined and synthesized.

Broadwood improved the stringing mechanism, designed a new scale and located the right striking point for the hammers. His

---

51. Rosen, C. "On Playing the Piano," *The New York Review of Books*, p.12

piano was more substantial in structure and sound. It resembled a harpsichord but was unevenly balanced between bass and treble. Indeed, its loud tone recalled the harpsichord. Its dampers, however, were not efficient, and it called for a deeper and cumbersome touch. By 1788 it had achieved greater sonority and evenness throughout the range, and increased dynamic flexibility. Its bass also had become rich and solid. It became a powerful underpinning, over which all kind of virtuoso and orchestral effects could be built. Jean Chrétien Bach became its first distinguished champion. Pleyel and Erard in Paris adopted his model, with modifications.

It was soon realized that Cristofori's escapement mechanism could be improved. In 1821, Sebastien Erard, an ingenious craftsman from Alsace, invented the "double escapement" — a mechanism for double repetition. Thanks to this innovation, the piano key is let up only about a third of its travel after a stroke, and any note can be repeated quickly without the hammer having to return fully to its highest level before being struck again, and without the damper touching the string between notes. Such repetition sounds not like a dull reiteration (as was the case with earlier versions), but as a controlled rhythmical emphasis. Thus, even before the finger moves, the hammer is already almost against the string and ready to strike. Erard's invention enabled very fast repetitions on the same key, and this was responsible for the effects of speed and glitter achieved by early pianists. It enlarged the performers' vocabulary and inspired virtuoso compositions like Liszt's Paganini studies.

From the very start, piano makers had to deal with two inter-related problems. First, they realized the need for soundboards. The vibrating string may contain all the partials but it is unable to radiate focused sound. However, soundboards are heavy. There was a danger that the string's vibration energy could be trapped within it and not be passed on to the air. One obvious solution was to use heavier strings with increased tension. This meant thicker and stiffer strings that added non-harmonic sounds and spoilt the desired piano timbres.

Piano designers got round the new problem in two ways, either by wrapping a rather thin steel core with copper, which also influenced the pitch, or by multiple stringing in which a thick plain string is split into two or three strings, tuned to almost the same frequency. They inserted two separate soundboards with connecting bridges for the two sets of strings.

Secondly, they had to find the optimal position for laying the strings. Traditional practices called for parallel lengths, but there were obvious advantages from crossing bass over treble. This procedure, called over-stringing, saved space. When they succeeded in working with only one soundboard, the bridges moved to its center, greatly intensifying the pitch.

The whole instrument was encased in a wooden frame. All innovation was spearheaded by the idea of obtaining sparkling pure sounds, and keeping out dissonant sounds. Even a slight adjustment in one part of the instrument had effects on other parts.

Until the 1770s, pianos were ambiguous instruments, transitional in construction and uncertain in status. Then the pace of technical progress quickened.

Soon, pianos with large keyboards appeared. Their outward appearance betrayed their harpsichord origins. The players now had access to a vast range of dynamics, including a gradual transition from one dynamic level to another. They could articulate contrast of dynamic levels not merely within the interior of the phrase but across the entire piece. Virtuosos reveled in the emphasis on contrast in piano music. When its potential was illustrated by the gradual *crescendo* over a full page or more of the score, it became clear that the piano was "the prince of instruments." Its sounds flashed with power and expressiveness. No other instrument could rival it in harmonic energy.

In 1779, Mozart obtained a five-octave piano made by Stein. He found its tone even and its damping clean. Then, in 1782, he created a series of masterpieces of concertos for the piano. In these, flowing, unembellished melodic lines compete and blend with the most lyrical of instruments like woodwinds and horns, and reflect the new mood in music. But Mozart was not a Romantic — his compositions do not express his feelings, but those of his characters.[52]

Beethoven enthusiastically adopted the new instrument, so unique among keyboard instruments. One of his contemporaries described the piano in these terms:

"It has the advantage that a finger's touch, heavy or light, determines the strength or the weakness of the sound; so it lends itself to the interpreter's expression as well as sentiment. From the touch, it receives a kind of magical life so that its sound can successively run through all the characters." Thus a new musical style suddenly burst on the artistic scene. Soon, "the piano, the interpreter of intimate thought, and normal instrument of domestic musical practice, came to dominate public musical life."[53]

Beethoven, in spite of his increasing deafness, immediately sensed that the relationship between piano and orchestra would change. In his Fourth Concerto he set the orchestra against the piano — but the outcome of the duel is uncertain. The soloist withdraws into a world so private that he seems oblivious of the aggressive outpourings of the orchestra.[54]

The symphony *Eroica*, played for the first time in Vienna in December 1804, ushers in the Romantic Revolution in music. "With the two opening chords, number three in E flat major, Beethoven thrust aside the old classical order with its precise rules, and opened the door to the glorious excesses of the Romantic era. If ever there was a moment that changed music, at least Western music, then this was it."[55] It was a historic leap, realized through sound. With him as never before, individual human aspirations, fears and

52. Gombrich, E.

53. Closson, E. *History of Piano*

54. Hopkins, A. *Understanding Music*

55. The Eroica, *The Economist*, Millennium Issue : Western classical music, Dec 23, 1999.

passions became central to music and threatened to overwhelm its structure.

In 1807, Beethoven acquired a grand piano and composed his Fifth Concerto, once again featuring a showdown between orchestra and piano. The orchestra music, marked by the absence of harmony, sounds aggressive. The piano replies with contemplative harmony, and triumphs. Its victory was to be long lasting.[56]

Liszt declared, "Perhaps this mysterious sentiment that attaches me to the piano is an illusion, but I consider its importance to be very great. In my view, the piano holds the first rank in the hierarchy of instruments, it is the most generally cultivated and most popular of all instruments. It owes its importance and popularity partly to the harmonic power it possesses; for this reason, it has the capacity to concentrate and sum up the entire art. In the space of its seven octaves, it embraces the range of an orchestra; and the ten fingers of a single man suffice to produce harmonies which otherwise need the concourse of more than a hundred concerted instruments. Thanks to its intervention, works, which the difficulties of putting together an orchestra would have left ignored or little known, are made known. It is to orchestral composition what engraving is to a picture: it multiplies, it transmits, and if it does not express colors, it at least discloses lights and shadows."[57]

Liszt initiated a tradition in which the piano sang and sparkled. He showed that the piano could imitate all the orchestra instruments. Indeed, he transformed virtuosity into liberty and freedom of movement. He was one of the first to enlarge the sound range of the piano, and to overhaul the technique of piano playing. With him the piano became, in turns, orchestra, harp, trumpet, or violoncello, and soberly articulated musical scales yielded their place to arabesque loops. He exploited every note of every octave, and explored all the registers from the solemn to the dashing. His

---

56. Hopkins, A.

57. Del Pueyo, *Entretiens sur le piano*, éditions Duculot

revolutionary technique inspired and continues to inspire numberless innovations, linked to the hand, in piano artistry. He swept away all academic taboos and reveled in fingerings that had been outlawed until then by the Classics.

With Liszt, the piano's victory over orchestra was complete. He composed for the piano, but he had orchestra in mind. His pieces, with their thunder of drums and blare of brass, celebrate the piano's triumph. They seem to proclaim that the piano can soar to heights beyond the reach of the orchestra.

Indeed, pianos changed rapidly and improved in quality. Those interpreting works for the evolving instrument sought to combine the possibilities of pianistic play with virtuosity. The public thronged to concerts, eager to see — or hear — what a performer could do with just ten fingers. What wonders the new virtuosos performed with the evolving keyboard! Now began an era of duels between virtuosos. One of the most famous was a concert featuring both Liszt and Thalberg. Parisian high society was divided; both the Hungarian and the Austrian had their fans.

"Thalberg is the best," claimed some — "but Liszt is unique."

A few years, later Schumann would make a correction: "Liszt is the best — *and* is unique. His talent is unrivalled in the world." And he was indeed the best, and in many ways unique.

One critic summed up the evening:

> Thalberg achieved everything that is possible to achieve by mechanical work. Inspiration and sentiment fail him and will always fail him. On the other hand connoisseurs admire in Liszt, above all, the wealth of harmony, the association and unfolding of ideas, the saintly melancholy of melodies and the freshness of brilliant passages.

By 1830, the grand piano emerged as a distinct instrument in its own right. Pianists were divided as to the virtues of the Viennese and English models. The first called for lighter action and gave clear and intimate sounds; but it could not compete in volume with the latter. Each model had its staunch supporters.[58]

In any case, the piano had certainly come to stay. Its basic repertoire was established. The lines of its future development were already traced out. Meanwhile, musicians were clamoring for bigger and brighter sounds...and the Romantic and Industrial Revolutions that erupted just then ushered in the golden age of the piano.

THE PIANO, A MARVEL OF MUSIC

The piano marked a decisive milestone in the development of Western music. It brushed aside the age-old tendency to look down on instruments as mere props for vocalists. Its richness of sounds and its capacity to realize dynamic nuances inspired a new style in keyboard music. From the instrument's very inception, the piano and piano music advanced hand in hand by mutual enrichment. Less than half a century following its invention, the piano established itself as the principal tool for music composition. It brought about a veritable revolution in the way people thought and felt about music.

And piano music, exploiting harmony and triads, is a spectacular development in the history of European art, unknown in other parts of the world. Piano music became the chosen field of experimentation for musicians. Such a paradigmatic change eventually led to Marie Jaëll's ventures into piano pedagogy.

Quality pianos were luxury goods in 1851, of course, and were rare. Produced by ingenious craftsmen following traditional lines, the standard was a square pianos shaped like a clavichord. Though they had acquired the modern tone, they had a narrower range than the instruments of today. In 1826, a year before his death, Beethoven wrote off the pianos of the time as inadequate, and called for "a heavier action, a sturdier instrument and a greater tone."

In the meanwhile the Romantic Movement in music had peaked. Its dream of making music the direct, concept-free

---

58. Bilson M., "The Viennese Fortepiano of the late 18th Century," *Early Music*, April 1980, 158-162

expression of emotion was coming true thanks to the piano, as an ecstatic Wagner was to observe. Under the piano's increasing dominance, the Romantics' urgency to convey personal sentiments paralleled the breakthrough of harmony as a positive force in music. Consequently, the emotional dimension of music came to the forefront in the world of art. By around 1830, the year of Berlioz's highly autobiographical *Symphonie Fantastique*, Romanticism had permeated pretty much all the arts. The compositions of new artists mirrored their deeply-lived personal dramas.

Indeed, as Romanticism extended its supremacy to all the domains of art, musicians began composing for the pianos of the future. Since the new instrument highlighted the beauty of individual sounds, they began to think vertically in order to exploit harmony. Their work, composed at the piano, clamored for more powerful instruments. Piano manufacturers stepped in and integrated the discoveries of scientific acoustics and the gadgets of industrial technology to build the modern piano. At the same time, they transformed piano manufacture into an industry and ushered in the golden age of piano. As the piano historian Ehrlich remarks, "great composers led, and piano-makers followed."[59]

A key intellectual input that went into the making of the piano was the science of sound. The Greeks were perhaps the earliest pioneers we know in this field; but where their innovations led could scarcely have been guessed. Pythagoras (ca. 566 — ca. 475 B.C.) is credited with having documented which notes sound pleasant or unpleasant to the human ear. Examining strings of different lengths but made of the same material, having the same thickness and under the same tension, he found their tones to be harmonious when the ratio of the lengths of string could be expressed in small whole numbers. By that system, the length ratio 2:1 sounds a musical octave, 3:2 a musical fifth and 4:3 a musical fourth.

---

59. Ehrlich, C. *The Piano, A History*

According to Greek acoustics, the most "consonant" interval was unison — when the same pitch was played or sung by two voices. The octave was the next most consonant, followed by the fifth and the fourth, while the other intervals became progressively more dissonant. By contrast, an extremely dissonant sound was produced when the octave was divided exactly in half. Such observations underlay early Western music that used almost exclusively the intervals of unison and octave. During the Middle Ages, the intervals of fifths and fourths were integrated. Renaissance musicians made the discovery of the major third, given by the ratio 5:4 — and they exploited it to build triads.

Then science took over and revolutionized the world of music. Mersenne proved the wave nature of sound, and measured its velocity to be 330 meters per second in dry air at 0° centigrade. He reworked the mathematical foundation of music, laid down by Pythagoras, in order to accommodate polyphony and new modes of consonance and dissonance. Newton had by then decomposed the color "white" into the chromatic spectrum, and imagined the tones of the musical scale to conform to the colors of a rainbow. Soon, three English acousticians — Noble, Pigot and Wallis — gave a scientific basis to his intuition and showed that when a note is sounded, other notes could be discerned in the vibrations provoked by it.

The new findings revealed that a single sound emitted by an instrument separates itself into harmonics. There was no need to look elsewhere for octaves and musical fourths and fifths. A single note contained them all. This confirmed the intuitive idea of the Western concept of harmony derived from the tonal spectrum. There is the fundamental tone, and a series of overtones or partials. The sound of individual overtones seems faint, almost inaudible, but it is their presence that gives luster to the overall sound. They determine the sound of an instrument.

The discovery that the foundations of harmony are derived from the components of sound itself was indeed revolutionary. As Schenker observes, "A piece of music became among other things a symbolic re-creation of the image of the relationship that exists in a single musical sound among the consonances of its overtone series." Such a vision of music haunted Marie Jaëll's work on rhythm as she sought to base her pedagogy on sure foundations.

The new insight into harmonics led to the creation of new resources for Western music. Foremost among them was tonality, or key, which lines up the notes, their own overtones and their octaves and other consonant notes. One note is suspended from a previous harmony in such a way as to create a feeling of tension. While two notes may be said to be in harmony, they cannot be committed to a tonality without the casting vote of a third note. In the new structure, one element in the chord, called the tonic note, is dominant over others. It indicates the overall melody, and the resulting hierarchy becomes a coherent and stable tonal system. Thus a tonality describes the relationships among constituent of melody and harmony: tones, intervals, chords scales and chromatic overtones. Music based on the harmonic system of chords was a spectacular development in European music since the Renaissance.

Paradoxically the new perspective endowed harmony with inbuilt movement. The material function of harmony is to confirm, deny or postpone arrival at a tonality. Its spiritual function is intimately concerned with the creation of emotion. It is two-faced and looks both backward and forward at the same time. It is remembrance and foresight, and creates reciprocity of succession among simultaneous relations. Most music establishes a tonic note that establishes a home from which the melody may start. Once again, such subtle observations under-gird Marie Jaëll's piano teaching for the "melody lead."

Twelve major keys and twelve minor keys encompass the marvels of musical scale formations. They originate in the irregular distribution of tones and semi-tones and the constant change of interval size. Since the seventeenth century the major keys have been associated with happiness, while the minor keys are understood to convey sadness. Chromatic intervals introducing notes that are foreign to the tonality are the most expressive. The harmonic structure in tonal music is so powerful that it reaches the emotional core of humans.

The discovery that Cristofori's instrument let musicians indulge in feats of harmony drove them forward. So long as music moved by relatively close non-chromatic intervals, there was no need to pay attention to harmony, and true intonation could be used. The advent of chromatic harmony forced them to deal with the age-old problem of tuning their instruments, as their fingers had to speed across entire octaves of the musical scale.

Already during the sixteenth century, Italian musical theory raised the problem of tuning. Renaissance musicians had invented a scale division called "mean tone temperament" that was accurately tabulated around 1562. By 1700 it was adopted all over Europe; but it rendered some keys unusable.

As composers began experimenting with harmony, the problem of tuning the entire musical system came to the fore. The keyboard instruments called for a fixed temperament. To meet the needs of the piano, the musicians hit upon the concept of "equal temperament," where the scale is divided into twelve equal semitones. In the new system the notes differed only slightly from natural harmonics. It caused a decisive difference in the language of music and enabled composers to open up all the resources of chromatic harmony and experiment with every tonality.

The new tuning system had a decisive impact on every aspect of music from the development of the sonata and the symphony to the design of instruments. It succeeded in respecting the proportions that govern the musical harmony and causing certain tones to vibrate together in order to produce a beautiful sound. For the first time, musicians could exploit every key, modulate from one to another, and yet preserve the keys' distinctive attributes. They could exploit harmonic regions distant from the main key in order to highlight the size of individual movements and their dramatic force.[60]

---

60. Rosen, *The New York Review of Books*

Equal temperament also gave the keyboard perfect musical symmetry. It helped tune each tone reliably equidistant from the ones that precede it and follow it. Thus a musical pattern, begun on one note, could be duplicated when starting on any other. Musicians also found that the piano's sonorous tone drowned out the slight dissonance of tempered intervals. As they began composing at the piano, they exploited to the full the complex relationships among the different keys and the freedom of modulation. Equal temperament was the wave of the future.

Indeed, the novel system of tuning underlay almost all Western music, especially after 1770. It was first incorporated in the Broadwood pianos in 1842. Immediately, musicians sensed the latent capabilities of the piano and found in it a rich acoustical palette of tonal colors for their use. As a result of this capacity, the piano is now the only keyboard instrument with which one can grandly vary the effects of the harmonics of a chord, at will, by balancing the sound in different ways. The new tuning system ushered in a novel musical universe.

In his "Letter on French Music," in 1753, Rousseau argued that music, rooted in the first cries of a baby and based on melody, was natural. He downgraded harmony-centered music as artificial. At the same time, scientific experiments were showing that vibrating objects emit overtones in addition to their primary tone — so that a close study of nature in fact revealed harmony to be the real basis of musical expression. Consequently Rameau, noting that nature favors harmony, defended equal temperament as the natural system since it alone allowed for harmonic movement across all the keys.

What is singular about harmony is that it is spatial — since the chord representing it is simultaneity and has only a dimension in space. But music flows in time and cries out for translation into a temporal sequence. Thus, harmony is always in a context and music cannot be just a succession of distinct sounds. Melody found a dynamic life in the new realm of harmony.

Also, a chord is more or less rich in sonority according to the way one brings to life the vibration of the harmonics of the underlying note. Therefore, beginning with the invention of the piano in the early eighteenth century, composers began to exploit the vibrations of the overtones in keyboard music. They sought to balance the vertical sound within a specific harmony with notes from low to high. Most of all, they excelled in the provision of vertical blocks of sound or in swift running passages. In this way they could convey constantly-varying degrees of tension so that emotion rose or fell with it.

When the piano became larger, in the nineteenth century, such exploitation became decisive in the hands of Chopin, Schumann and Liszt. They used the sustaining pedal not as a special effect (as in Haydn and still in Beethoven) but as a continuous vibration added to the sound. With the gradual development of the fashion for public concerts, their innovation helped carry the sound farther in larger performance spaces.

During this evolutionary period, musicians worked to transfer the known resources of vocal music to the piano. For singing purposes, where there is a need for a consistent and positive rhythmic pulse, vowels are more useful to sustain a sound and to prolong syllables. When there is accompaniment for vocal music, a built-in tension occurs between the slow-moving voice and the more dynamic rhythms of the instrumental music. Such a handicap had a restricting effect on the development of rhythm as an independent force.

Bach claimed that vocal music was reproduced properly only when performed as if it were instrumental, and instrumental music should be performed as if it were vocal — i.e. as is if it were speaking, with the forcefulness of speech.[61] Handel found a solution by treating the voice more as an instrument than as a bearer of a verbal message. In the components of an instrumental piece like the sonata and symphony, as created by Mozart and Haydn, the melodic line is still essentially vocal in conception; the natural stress and

---

61. Georgiades, T. *Music and Language* (translated by Göllner M.L.) Cambridge University Press 1982, p. 77.

accent correspond to the syllables of a phrase. By contrast, the instrumental concept is found in display passages full of swift running scales, brilliant arpeggio chains of 3^{rds} or 6^{ths} and so on, which would be beyond the capabilities of even the most gifted singer. Gradually, instrumental music broke loose from its dependence on vocal music.

The opera suggested another solution to piano's intrinsic deficiency. In it, the solo singer's expressive phrases were accompanied by relatively static harmonies. These were selected with considerable subtlety in order to bring out the emotional content of the words they accompanied. They created tensions by associating to the profoundly expressive vocal lines in marked dissonance against the supporting chords. Inspired by such devices, composers attempted to line up consonance against dissonance to provoke emotions. They enlarged the riches of tonality to capture the sense of musical flow across phrases through the build-up and release of tension. Consonant tuning was supplanted in its coordinating role by unstable dissonant tuning.

A better solution, however, appeared from within the characteristics of piano itself. The piano lacks the sustaining qualities of wind and string instruments and the human voice. As soon as a chord is played, it begins to fade away. No amount of pressure will prolong it. To overcome this inherent weakness, musicians invented the device of repeated chords. These give artificial respiration to sounds in danger of extinction.

Ironically, the technique of repeated chords, initially designed to give life to harmony, helped renew rhythmic vitality. The musicians first introduced silences or syncopations to break the regularity of chord patterns. They found quick, repeated chords to be exciting, whereas slowly repeated chords were restful if quiet, majestic if loud. Thus, led by Liszt, they enthusiastically embraced the technique of repeated chords and a to-and-fro rocking of the components of a chord as pulse beats to enliven their music. Thus, rhythm took on an independent life. Such musical innovation was the context for Erard's technical invention of the "double escapement" mechanism that facilitated very fast repetition of the same key without the damper touching the string in between the notes.

Berlioz and Liszt reveled in the use of throbbing repeated chords at moments of high passion. They were also most inventive in the exploitation of irregular rhythms. Liszt's dramatic ingenuity is most evident in a passage of *Reminiscences of Don Juan*, where a cascade of chromatic octaves alternates with single notes in a spectacular way. The repeated chord techniques found consecration in the most passionate outbursts of the musical pieces of Wagner and Schumann. All the composers, as true Romantics, turned to Nature for inspiration and integrated in their musical pieces many of the repetitive patterns present, there like the recurring ocean waves, the delicate tracery of veins upon a leaf and the geometric symmetry of snow-crystals. By this means they realized the Romantic vision of Art imitating Nature. Marie Jaëll, as she developed her novel piano pedagogy, subjected nature's rhythms to a close scrutiny in order to invest piano play with a sense of motion.

More importantly, musicians combined the technique of repeated chords with the differing qualities of consonance and dissonance in order to express subtler aspects of emotion. They conveyed tension through an unstable interval, and then resolved it by sliding to a more acceptable note. They expressed joys and sorrows by transitions across major and minor intervals. Their innovation breathed pathos and a sense of unease into music that released intense emotions.

Such disturbances, combined with rhythm, became integral to piano music in order to convey messages. Consequently, piano-inspired music was moving in two ways, one by the motive power of rhythm, and the other by tension created by dissonance and resolved by consonance. The contours of tension and release are defined by changes from dissonant to consonant chords, from non-accented to accented notes, from higher to lower notes and from prolonged to non-prolonged notes.

Curiously, the piano helped reveal the mysterious union between music and emotion. Recent neuroscience research has unearthed a deep link between patterns of musical intervals and patterns of emotion. The brain areas involved in emotional processing in response to consonance and dissonance melodies are separate from the auditory cortex.[62] Recognition of music and its emotional appreciation use different neural pathways. It would seem that the human brain strings together the notes of a melody as if they were a stream of sound, but pays attention to harmonic relations among them. The ear receives a jumbled cacophony of sounds and the inner ear dissects a sound into its component frequencies. In a sense, it seems that the brain guesses the simultaneous sounds in harmonic relations to be the overtones of a single sound, groups them, then glues them together and perceives them as forming a complex tone.

Musicians also discovered that the piano could provide the semblance of a continuum of sound. Naturally, they exploited such a property to emphasize dynamic contrasts and introduce a gradual transition from one dynamic level to another. Such transitions existed before the second half of the eighteenth century; but they were expressive within the interior of a phrase. With the piano they became structural, and helped articulate lengthy patterns.

The piano is the only keyboard instrument in which one can grandly vary the effects of the harmonics of a chord, at will, by balancing the sound in different ways. In addition, the sustaining right foot pedal can be used to activate all the tones simultaneously, in order to emphasize the harmonic dimension of music. Other instruments, like the violin, the cello, the flute and the oboe, cannot rival the piano in the sheer volume of sound or in its enhanced capacity for sustaining and projecting them. They cannot compete with its great sonority, especially its ability to realize dynamic nuances and an entire score on its own revolutionized music

---

62. Zatorre, *Nature*, March 7, 2002

composition. Thus composers, as they began to experiment in the expression of personal emotions, found a powerful ally in the piano.

But the Cartesian mind-body dichotomy once again acted as brake on musicians wanting to compose at the piano. Prejudices were rampant: it was thought that a piece of music should be first conceived as an abstract form and not directly in material sound. Some argued that a gifted composer did not need to lean on the crutch of a keyboard for his creation. There were also musicians who maintained that vocal harmony could not be worked out on the piano keyboard, since vocal intonation and piano tuning belong to two different worlds of music and, unlike a singer, a pianist cannot inflect the intonation of a note in mid-phrase. Nonetheless, in spite of such fixed ideas, the practice of composing at the piano gained ground and soon became the norm.

Composers "think sound" as sculptors and painters "think forms." According to the Romantics, musical creation takes place in the subconscious. Sounds surface to the consciousness, sometimes sharply defined, sometimes obscure, and as they bubble up, they assume coherent shapes. In this manner the musical substance takes on life.

Composers have also to be experts in the manipulation of musical language. They need to have an inborn sense of tonal relationships. They have to master notes and their organization. If emotion plays too dominant a part, intellect may lose control; if intellect plays too great a part, the resulting music may be dry.

Also, each musical instrument has its own feel and, to a certain extent, dictates the structure of the music to be played on it. Composers grope for the right notes and give directions to guide performers. The association between an instrument and the music ideally written for it is something that a performer should learn first. Music comes to full life only on the instrument for which the composer intended it.

Mozart composed for a five-octave piano and his music soars to sublime heights only when played on such instruments. Chopin's lyrical music is most haunting on the medium-sized pianos for which he composed. Liszt and Schumann had access to larger pianos, and they excelled in exploiting the vibrations of the overtones of piano sounds.

The first pieces composed for the piano were Bach's two Fugues in his *Musical Offering*. His works exploit the fundamentals of the tonality language, and so sound best on the piano. Joseph Haydn (1732-1809) is one composer whose active life spanned the time from the piano's emergence to its leap to pre-eminence. In his early days he composed for clavichord and harpsichord, but when the first pianos appeared on the scene, he happily wrote for them. In his *Grand Sonata*, composed in 1800 for the pianoforte, he fully exploited the power and scope of the new instrument. His compositions, though of keyboard conception, recall orchestral sounds.

Tradition has it that Mozart composed in his head, away from the piano. In fact, he "worked out his ideas at the piano, and only then did he sit down and write." However, the greatest interaction between piano and the process of composition begins with Beethoven. As early as 1796, he sensed the musical potential of the new instrument. A new grand come into his possession in 1807, at the very moment his aural faculties were failing. He sawed its legs off and played it on the floor, in order to feel its vibrations. He could also count on the limitless repertoire of phrases and motifs that he had learnt in his younger days. His responses to the questions of piano manufacturers and his recommendations played a critical role in piano production.

Schumann's first decade as a composer was almost entirely devoted to piano music. Apparently, he was unhappy at his dependence on the piano for composition, especially when testing the relation between the voice and the piano. Chopin wrote almost exclusively for the piano. His originality partly stems from his exploitation of piano sonority to achieve a synthesis of different styles and to combine the lyrical melody of Italian opera with the polyphonic riches of Johann Sebastian Bach. His mature works display a delicate balance between virtuosity and emotional force. Both he and Schumann arranged the accompanying harmonies to make the notes of the melody vibrate. Debussy was to exploit the same techniques and create extraordinary effects.

Music inspiDebussyred by the piano took Beethoven's *Eroica* for its model. It is structured around harmony. Its forms are processes simulating time and giving the impression of dynamic time.[63]

Berlioz was one conspicuous exception; he really did compose away from the piano. He even boasted that his inability to play the piano saved him from the "terrible influence" of the keyboard style. In truth, his incompetence at the piano prevented him from securing employment at the Paris Conservatory of Music.

The forms of instrumental music include Preludes, Fugues, Sonata, Symphonies and Concertos.[64] Beethoven began with the piano sonata, moved on to the symphony and consolidated his experience with the string quartet. Most composers have followed the same sequence.

Preludes allowed musicians to escape from metric constraints and enabled instrumental music to develop independently. A typical prelude by Bach is primarily conceived in term of harmonies.

Fugues are essentially linear in concept. They always begin with a single line expressing a melodic idea, and then gain in density. Bach was a supreme master of the form. Beethoven liked them for their texture. But, they lost favor with Romantics who delighted in harmonies.

"Variations" are constructed around a few fundamentals: a sound, an easily recognizable structure and a tune with one or two identifiable characteristics. The sonata is a musical form that exploits relationships among the different keys that was such a potent force in Romantic music.

The symphony is basically a sonata for an orchestra. Three composers stand out: J. C. Bach, Haydn, and Beethoven. With his

---

63. Brinlmann, R., "In the Time(s) of the 'Eroica'", p.8

64. Hopkins A., *Understanding Music*.

104 symphonies, Haydn developed the form extensively. Beethoven composed nine symphonies: in the first two he follows the Haydn model, in the third he breaks through to a new pattern and in the last four he abandons the Classical straitjacket and moves towards the Romantic and subjective approach. In his wake, the symphony became an intellectual challenge to composers as well to the audience, since it demanded a feat of concentration.

The "concerto" is another elaboration of the sonata, with the presence of a soloist. It came into its own with the piano. As the piano developed more power, the hero figure could take on his adversaries with ever-greater confidence. With the arrival of brilliant solo keyboard performers, piano concertos became theaters for flights of fancy.

Curiously, some of the most "orchestral" music of the piano repertory was composed before the modern piano was invented. Early composers fully exploited the musical capabilities of their pianos, and wrote for future instruments with newer qualities. For example Beethoven's *Waldstein*, *Appassionata* and *Les Adieux* sonatas display successive increases in piano compass. For his Opus 106, he needed a piano with six and a half octaves. A little later, Chopin and Liszt had access to pianos with full seven octaves. Then came Schumann's *Fantasia* (1836), Liszt's *Sonata* (1853) and Brahms' First Concerto (1858), all of which demanded greater power and tonal range. "Even a steely modern Steinway can barely stand up to the demands of this monumental music, with its pummeling chords, gnashing trills and hell-bent final fugue."

The new music called for a new generation of instruments, and a new generation of manufacturers stepped in. Conversant with the techniques introduced by the Industrial Revolution then in full swing, they took full advantage of the technical progress in metallurgy and the new science of acoustics. Three manufacturers, Steinway in New York, Bechstein in Berlin and Blüthner in Leipzig led way in 1853 and transformed piano manufacture into a flourishing industry. Unfortunately Erard and Pleyel, once dynamic

French manufacturers, were content to follow rather than initiate changes.

As highlighted earlier, the dynamics of piano making was driven from the very start by the search for unalloyed sounds. To meet the new needs, piano manufacturers gradually increased the weight and tension of strings. Now the piano's load-bearing structure, made entirely of wood, was too fragile and could not support the increased stresses. Indeed, in the pianos built before 1860 the strings broke frequently, and the top octave degenerated into a wooden knock.

The piano makers tried integrate new technologies into their instrument. They soon learnt to combine scientific results, engineering and musical sensitivity. They installed heavier strings under great tension and used metal struts to brace the casework. But such changes greatly augmented the strain on the instrument's frame. So they adopted the iron frame, cast in one piece and covered with wood.

Cast iron frames soon became the norm; then the manufacturers concentrated their ingenuity on the hammers and strings. Thus in addition to the mechanical skills necessary to come up with a good piano design, they had to master acoustics, a science in its infancy at the time. Helmholtz's book *On the Sensation of Tone*, published in 1862, was the first book to deal explicitly with the problem. He analyses systematically the relationships between the sound produced by of musical instruments and its perception by the ear. Though his measuring equipment was simple, his results on the tonal characteristics of piano guided manufacturers in their choice of strings.

The hammers, which play a decisive role in determining the tone quality and largely define the instrument, also benefited from the technical progress. In Cristofori's model, they were of the same size. In the newer pianos, their size and weight increased as one moved from treble to bass in order to achieve the best compromise between tone quality, loudness and playability. They were also covered with felt or leather in order to assure a smooth, silent motion free from backlash. Heavier hammers stay longer in contact with the strings. The duration of contact time diminishes from bass to treble mainly as a result of the decreasing hammer mass.

Piano makers today choose metal strings with great care; different lengths and thicknesses assure the required gradations from bass to treble. They use thicker strings, two or three for each note, at high tensions. They favor steel wire for the treble, and steel over-spun with copper for the bass. The position along the string where the hammer strikes is equally important, in order to prevent dissonant overtones like the seventh, ninth and tenth, and retain only the consonant overtones.

The final major innovation concerned an efficient transfer of vibration energy of the strings to the soundboard. The first upright pianos in which the bass strings crossed the others in a fan-like pattern were built in 1863. This became the model for all later instruments of quality. The resulting soundboard radiates sounds much better than the strings. But in its construction there is a trade off to be made between loudness and duration of sound. If the soundboard is thicker, the piano sounds are louder but their duration is shorter. To arrive at the optimal compromise between loudness and sustaining power, an engineer turned to multiple stringing.

There were numerous other innovations, inspired by the music that was being written and resulting from patient experimentation and great elementary knowledge. One was the strengthening of the strings' resistance to the hammer blows. Most significant was the duplex scale, with its tone even more liquid, singing and harmonious. Over-stringing, which some thought would lead to unevenness, turned out to be an important breakthrough and Helmholtz, in admiration of the innovations, noted that "the tone throughout the entire scaling [was] remarkable for its evenness and its wonderful sweetness, richness and volume."

The modern piano could not have come into being but for the Industrial Revolution. "In the voluminous reports of the industrial congresses held in the Crystal Palace in London from 1851 to 1914, the concert grand piano received more coverage than any other item of manufacture, including locomotives and steam turbines."[65] But more than a feat of engineering, the piano was a marvel of music. In spite of all the industrial inputs, piano making is essentially the work of artisans. With 12,000 components and eight different woods including maple, birch, spruce and poplar, it takes almost a year of skilled work to build a Steinway.

By 1860, the piano had acquired its modern form, the compass of seven octaves and great structural and tonal strength. Iron-framed pianos gave the player a new range of dynamic and a wider range of colors. The innovations decisively enhanced the tone. The greatly increased thickness and tension of the strings added strength and brilliance, particularly in the treble. In this way they obtained not merely correct pitches but also a smooth transition in tone quality throughout the register. Pianists now control unprecedented power.

Most of the leading French composers, like Berlioz, Saint-Saëns, and Gounod, addressed compliments to Steinway. Both Liszt and Wagner heaped the most fulsome encomiums on the new piano. Berlioz, familiar with the instrument's resources, declared that the Steinway piano had reached a point of perfection and could outdo all other instruments in the production of overtones. Its main attractions lay in its splendid and noble sonority, and its virtual elimination of the terrible resonance of the minor seventh.[66]

The principle of piano's functioning is indeed simple. The pianist "touches" the key; a felt hammer strikes a metal string that is connected to a large wooden plate. The string is set in vibration by the impact, and the vibrations are transferred to the soundboard that radiates the sound.

However, an exact description of the production of piano sound is not yet available, since it is difficult to master the physics of

65. Piano Man, The New York Review of Books, footnote.

66. Ehrlich, C., A History of the Piano

the different steps involved — the collision of the hammer with the string, the transmission of the string vibrations to the soundboard, and the radiation of the sound from the soundboard. Moreover, "simple" materials like felt and wood seem to have highly complex properties and add to the intricacy of the phenomena.

The difference of the shape and amplitude of the force pulse generated at the impact is determined by the final hammer velocity and by a combination of the mechanical properties of the hammer's head. The hammers are designed so as to make the force pulse shorter in the treble than in the bass. Thus, a harder blow yields a larger amplitude and sharper corners to the pulse on the string. The piano tone will contain a more brilliant tone quality at *forte* compared to *piano*.

Cristofori had called his invention piano *and* forte, since one could vary its dynamic level. As his creation reached perfection, one could play it piano and forte *at the same time!* This is the true miracle of the modern piano. Indeed, more than a marvel of engineering, the piano is the marvel of music.

Some musicians were nostalgic. They were fond of their earlier instruments, stamped with strong individual qualities. There is no doubt that "pianos built before the twentieth century frequently displayed intentionally wide ranges of tone color." Early instruments were known for their quickly decaying sounds with crystalline transparency. In contrast, the modern piano produced robust, long-sustaining and fundamentally rich sounds. The industrial age, carried forward by its logic of mass production, imposed the ideal of a standardized piano with perfect evenness throughout its range.

With the modern piano, Schumann's ambition came true. He always dreamt of a musical instrument that dispensed with the verbal intrusion between music and its meaning, and permitted the immediacy of action on emotion. Though a poet himself, he disliked the inherent ambiguity of words. He believed that authentic music fills the soul better than words. Truly, piano music, seemingly unfiltered through a web of meanings, works most directly on the chords of emotion, and communicates nothing but formless emotions. Its power stems from its decisive de-linking from words. Thus the Western vision of music as a vehicle of ideas composed for the purpose of penetrating man's mind found its ultimate fulfillment in the piano.

The piano disclosed a new vision of pure music existing by itself, without any outside reference and without scenic or literary support. Its music had a meaning simply constructed with, and derived from, the very elements of expression. Its notes called attention to themselves. The meaning now was in the notes themselves, not in what they purported to say. The over-arching form of a musical piece can be apprehended in its totality only in terms of its sonorous elements realizing their unity. The tonal system helped reach that goal.

In a startling way, the piano music restored the primeval tie between music and magic. Indeed, it seems to signal that the roots of music have a more ancient origin than human language. It is found that people who live close to nature perceive a wider range of sounds[67] than those who are forced to make a living in noisy and polluted modern towns. To the latter, the piano, a marvel of technology, gives access to a paradise they have lost.

Thus, an in-depth analysis of harmony discloses why Romantic music expresses itself best through the modern piano, a product of modern engineering. Naturally, the Romantic artists ranked piano music highest among the arts because of its stirring power. In it they could express so much meaning and emotions that trespass the realms of rationality. However, the artistic value of a piano piece is not determined by its impact on sentiments alone, but by its ability to unlock the doors of a spiritual kingdom.

In Marie Jaëll's view, the temperament of an instrument is finally far less interesting than the temperament of a musician. Her piano pedagogy insists that a beautiful tone color depends on the

---

67. Gray P.M et al., "The Music of Nature and the Nature of Music," *Science*, January 5, 2001 :52-54

harmonic significance of the notes. According to her, the pianist must learn the graceful resolution of the expressive harmonies. For the creation of beautiful sounds, he needs first to sense the underlying rhythm of the musical piece

One composer with whom piano became sovereign was Debussy. Like Liszt, he treated the piano as a surrogate orchestra, but his attitude was different. His piano pieces do not proclaim the piano's triumph over other instruments but quietly celebrate its supremacy. Debussy tried his first radical attempts at harmony at the piano. He exploited the exceptional resources of the instrument to achieve a happy precision of sensation. He took for his motto, "Let's invent our fingerings; anything goes when it comes to obtaining the right sound effect." And his sounds are so right for the piano. No other instrument can render their quiet power. "Verticality, characteristic of harmony, found its final triumph in his music. It is the harmony of mystery."[68]

Above all, Debussy's music is visual. Hopkins notes that Debussy, in his musical piece "*Reflets dans l'eau,*" takes the sounds and movements of nature and bends them to his will. "The entire piece takes less than five minutes to play and yet in that time a huge storm brews up, raising immense waves such as few lakes have ever known, only to die down to an evening of immense stillness and beauty."[69] His music takes aspects of our immediate experience and reworks them, reflecting them back in altered form. It relates to the immediacy of everyday life — but not immediately, a key feature of great art. Other paradoxes characterize his work. As Jankélévitch remarks, an intra-musical silence bathes all his music as if silence is the inmost core of all music. Truly, in Debussy, "Music learnt to speak softly."

The piano realized the Romantic dream of creating pure music, existing by itself and outside of all action, stripped of all scenic and literary argument. It could not have into existence but for the

---

68. Debussy, Cortot, p.9
69. Hopkins A., *Understanding Music*, p.180.

development of the science of sound, the introduction of the tonal system and above all the technological breakthroughs of the Industrial Revolution. The entire thrust of Marie Jaëll's pedagogy is to tap such depths in piano music.

THE HYPOSTASIS OF THE PIANO

...In memory of the one who gave me this book, I will continue to write. Ten years ago he asked me to note down my thoughts every day...

After many years' silence, Marie Jaëll finally recovered her taste for writing. She took up the big notebook Liszt had offered her as a gift and started jotting down a few lines daily, as he had counseled her to do.

In 1893, a new life beckoned her. Her personality blossomed, and she was brimming with energy. Her self-doubts seem to have melted away. She had a clear view of the path that she would pursue unswervingly. At long last, she intuited the true significance of all her questionings. With lucidity she sensed the direction her research had taken:

I am surprised at my blindness. I have spent my life clearing the path without noticing what lay in front of me, groping all the time, and believing I was distant from the goal.

Truly, I have been possessed by this intense consuming rage for progress; this is, indeed, the magnet that has attracted me to the point where I am now. And to acknowledge that it has taken me ten years! How could I have been blind so long?

"I cannot be satisfied with intuition, I must understand," she explained to one of her friends. In these words, scribbled down with passion on a sheet of paper, she summed up her life's mission.

Before plunging into the work that would absorb her life so much so that the world would gradually move away from her, she felt she was duty-bound to pay a last homage to her friend Liszt. She therefore gave a series of concerts, and played his entire *oeuvre* for the piano. Few pianists had taken up such a daunting challenge! Her performance sparked wide interest, and the concerts were an unqualified success. An ecstatic Saint-Saëns exclaimed, "There is only one person who can play Liszt, and that is Marie Jaëll."

Then, in the following year, she gave a concert performance of the complete ensemble of Beethoven's sonatas for the piano. In Paris, she was the first person to play his thirty-two sonatas, "the most prestigious work in the solo piano literature." "Marie Jaëll, a distinguished pianist," the 1893 press reports read, "has single-handedly taken up six soirées of the big Pleyel salons in the season with which we are concerned. They have been unforgettable to the most earnest lovers of good music. Mme Jaëll is the artist of bold initiatives."

For one more year Marie, in full possession of her faculties and at the pinnacle of her art, continued to give concerts. Then, abruptly, she gave up playing in public, abandoned composing, and withdrew from the public.

What were the forces at work in her inmost depths at this moment?

It would seem she was finally ready to take up the mission she felt destiny had ordained for her. As a virtual alchemist, she was going to tap the secrets of musical art and the mysteries of the pianistic touch, and to orient her research towards piano sonority and technique. In the silence of her Parisian apartment in *rue Tournon*, she felt emboldened to formulate an original method of piano teaching. Soon she published a first version of it, giving it the title, "The Touch." It was to be an overture to an ambitious program.

This was the first time "touch" was used in the piano context. It is true that Bach had used the word in 1710, urging musicians to carefully develop the touch of the clavichord. François Couperin "*L'Art de Toucher le Clavecin*," published in 1717, is a technical treatise that explains how to draw singing sounds from the harpsichord, how to give the sounds life in order to render the music expressive. Chopin's system of fingering and touch was derived from the eighteenth century tradition that was based on the differing strengths and capabilities of each finger. In contrast, Marie Jaëll's book is permeated by a penetrating analysis of piano sounds and an overarching philosophy of music.

She entered the fray just as a battle was raging among pianists concerning the attitude they should adopt towards their instrument. They were sure of piano's secure place in the world of music; their debate focused on the best piano pedagogy.

Music lovers were embracing the piano in its final form as a gift from heaven. Its pure sounds evoked boundless fascination among composers, performers and concert-goers. By the close of the nineteenth century, the intimate pianoforte of eighteenth century salons had developed into a sonorous instrument, an orchestra in and of itself, rich in timbres and harmonics. Its ability to allow the different voices to interpenetrate each other was enthralling. Pianists were in awe of their instrument; but a split had occurred among them as early as 1830, when the pianos were becoming increasingly more powerful and highly developed.

Some exploited it as an expressive instrument. Some others only sought to dazzle audiences by their speed and power. Even in 1890, as Bauer remarks, "the perfection of the instrument inclined them to lessen the study of a good tone. Pianists expected mechanical infallibility, which relieved them of having to learn how the machine worked at all. This defect was due to the ignorance of pianists in regard to the construction of this instrument. In the past the performer treated his instrument as a respected and beloved friend; many of our present performers appear to treat it as an enemy who has to be fought."[70]

Thus the conflict centered on the question of finding the best relationship between the pianist and his instrument. Musicians did not have a full grasp of the complex aesthetics that govern the dynamics of the musicality of the piano. Liszt himself, though he marveled at the magnificence of the volume and quality of piano

---

70. Bauer

sounds, confessed his ignorance of the piano's mechanics. To all, it was evident that the piano, as a technological product, demanded a precise understanding on the part of the performer. But what gripped the audience's attention most was the pianist's technical prowess. Thus a gap between musical expression and technical resources appeared, and it seemed to be widening. This was a challenge to the pianists.

They took time to size up the vast potential of their beloved instrument. With the clavichord, touch was everything, for it was direct and one played from the surface of the keys at their forward ends. The performer did not need to engage his muscles. He had to concentrate on having a delicate and intimate control in order to obtain a sensitive gradation of tone along with intensity and quality of sound. The harpsichord, on the other hand, was sufficiently loud and brilliant; but the player could not directly master the force on the string, and so he could not produce subtle changes in volume.

As musicians sensed the radical difference between the old instruments and the piano, new styles of piano playing gradually appeared. At first, performers were content with an exclusively digital technique. Then they extended their efforts to fingers, wrists and forearms, but still holding the elbows immobile and tucked into the body. Saint-Saëns observed that such techniques did not suffice to play Liszt's compositions.

In quest of greater power and dexterity, later developments encouraged freedom in the upper arms and shoulders. But Liszt's way of exploiting octaves also mobilized the back and shoulder muscles. And when applied to Berlioz's music, these techniques brought into action all the muscular effort of the performer. Such dynamics of piano playing led directly to the emergence of "superman" piano virtuosos.

Indeed, the piano was a revolutionary instrument. The graceful or dramatic movements of the arms and twists of the performer have no practical effects on the mechanism of the instrument. It is constructed in such a way that a single note can only be played more or less *forte* or *piano*. The elaborate arrangements of joints and springs within the instrument are such that the hammer strikes the strings with greater or lesser force. As Rosen remarks, "there is no such thing as playing the piano more or less beautifully."[71]

Thus, playing the piano is fundamentally different from playing string instruments. The string players are in physical contact with the string, through their fingers, so that their instruments are almost like an extension of their limbs. They can continuously feed it with energy, and control the tone as long as the note sounds. In contrast a piano, with its steel frame, is so much greater than a violin or a flute in size that a pianist almost has to become part of his instrument in order to master it. Indeed, he has to merge with it as he works himself up to strike the *fortissimo* with the greatest intensity.

Thus, it is not surprising that a pianist resembles a singer and gives the impression of having internalized his instrument, so as to dominate its sound from within. In this way he transforms himself also into a string player, and participates directly in the creation of the volume of sound. His entire being vibrates at the slightest increase in the sound he produces on his piano. He literally feels the music's power in all his muscles, as he has to cooperate directly in every *crescendo* and *decrescendo*. To a greater extent than violinists or other instrumentalists, a pianist enters into the full harmonic texture of the music as he plays the piano.

It slowly dawned on pianists that their music now mobilized their whole personality. They realized that it was not enough to bring in line all the muscular effort of their bodies. A new perspective appeared and asked the pianist to bring in line his entire being, so that it experienced the music he played and its emotional content coalesced with his physical expression. "The danger of the piano and its glory is that the pianist can feel the music with his whole body without having to listen to it."[72]

Strangely, such an unusual perspective on recalls music's origin in dance. "Music is the floor on which people dance." It always

71. Rosen, C., "Playing the Piano," *The New York Review of Books*

72. Rosen, C., *Ibidem*, p.12

suggests movement, and taps into the system of motor control. People shake and swing, clap and snap to music. Also, repetitive rhythms, rooted in bodily movements, underlie much of instrumental music. In piano as in dance, there has to be muscle control in order to dominate sequences of tensions and their release. In both, movements are carried out with urgency and enthusiasm or lassitude and submission, so that erect or slumping body postures reflect confidence or depression. Both contain a concentrated dose of stimulus to pleasure. Curiously, successful pianists are no different from great actors who have learnt to control all their muscles in a highly coordinated way and to mobilize both body and mind to express emotion.

Piano music may be a delight to hear, but producing it is no easy task. Indeed, the technical prowess of piano playing is a form of sport. Already in 1675, Scarlatti had called the keyboard performance of his early sonatas a sport as well as an art. It takes several years of training to master the technical dimension. From this point of view, the vocations of a pianist, a dancer, an actor and an athlete are all alike.

Those who want to be leaders in piano music need to undergo explicit training and extensive practice, just as in tennis, athleticism, mountaineering and fencing. They also have to submit to tiresome, taxing, exhausting routines over long periods, with arduous repetition of passage after passage.

Pianists, as they tried to learn Liszt's technique of playing the octave passages, also found that they had to endure physical pain. It was conjectured at the time that "the hours of practicing parallel octaves were the reason why so many pianists lost control of the four and fifth fingers of their right hands." Pianists hit upon a constant rhythmic pattern as an optimal way to time the movements. But in such bravado playing, there was a danger that physical endurance and strength would take precedence over musicality as they displayed astonishing leaps of crossing of hands and rapid repeated notes.

It is also true that both artists and sportsmen end up cultivating a genuine love for the mechanics and take pride in the difficulties they encounter during their exercises in order to excel in their chosen field. They may even revel in the exhilaration of violence that is an essential component of athletics, dance and musical performance at the highest level.

Pianists find a certain pleasure in exhibiting showmanship. They are proud to display their physical prowess. Their bodies communicate movement, speed, and strength as well as emotion and pain. The way they surmount technical difficulties is often expressive. The audiences go into raptures on seeing the power of piano players. But they can hardly guess the discomfort and anguish the latter endure to reach the pinnacle of their art — or sport.

As pianos became capable of greater performance, musicians were increasingly convinced of the necessity to undergo special and painful training and submit to long hours of practice, especially to take full advantage of the octave effects. Different schools sprang to life and proposed techniques to educate the fingers for piano action. There was a fair measure of mystique and still much disagreement on what ought to be the right technique.

A danger soon appeared that musical interpretation would branch off in the direction of pure physical display. The first pianos did not provoke any virtuosity. Indeed, there was a certain loss of it in Haydn and Mozart. Musicians were just taking the measure of their new instrument. As the pianos gained enormously in sonority and responsiveness and musicians gained control of their instrument, the era of flashy virtuosity took off. Soon pianists were no longer interpreters but were respected as soloists. "Nothing is impossible for man," remarks Jankélévitch about the piano of this epoch, "you are going to see, ladies and gentlemen, what a man can do with his ten fingers, all that a virtuoso can do with his keyboard; you are going to see what a man can do alone."

Liszt, the peerless pianist, led the way with startling individual feats at the piano in an age of public music. He inaugurated a new era in keyboard technique, and fathered a tradition in which the pianos sang and sparkled. In his hands, at least, they were capable of imitating all the instruments of the orchestra. His virtuoso showmanship and physical excitement enraptured audiences.

Unfortunately, the infatuation with piano virtuosity led interpreters astray from the true musical sense, and it had a baleful impact on piano teaching. The drive to produce virtuosos at all costs dominated piano pedagogy. All efforts were concentrated on the artificial training of hands and fingers. The cult of the child prodigy went hand in hand with adulation of flashy virtuosity. It was the heyday of diabolical machines invented in order to render the fingers suppler and stronger. Schumann was one of their unhappy victims. After using one of them in order to stretch the tendons that would give him a wider reach across the keyboard, his right hand was struck by partial paralysis from which he never recovered.

The piano as a sound machine was being detoured from its greatest mission. One school of pedagogy argued that it did not matter if it were a finger or the end of a broomstick that struck the key. Taking the training of animals as a model, it suggested automatic repetition to learn clever fingering. Kalkbrenner, a professor at the time, wrote, "life is too short for a true artist to learn what is indispensable to know, without some clever means to cheat time. He is compelled to read, while doing the exercises." The obsession with agile manipulations and mere skill meant that the piano as an instrument took precedence over music *per se*. Thus began a tradition of performance that replaced inspired interpretation by mechanical jugglery.

It was a depressing denial of art! Already Beethoven had remarked (speaking of the pianists of his day), "the speed of their fingers puts their intelligence to flight." Luckily, musicians of the stature of Liszt and Chopin, pianists above all, stepped in, reinvented the piano and gave it back its splendor.

Liszt was quite unhappy at the way piano was being taught, almost everywhere, in his day. He wrote to one of his friends, "By following the traditional bad ways, one only succeeds in turning out legions of dull automatons. We must resolutely appeal to the intelligence of both pupils and masters to devote the noblest faculties of the human soul to the exercise of mechanics." Chopin's conception of technique placed the contrast of touch at the center of musical interpretation. In his music the most delicate passages are to be played with fingers alone.

Thanks to the intervention of leading pianists, piano music took on a fresh meaning and was enriched. They argued that technique, though essential, is only a means to an end, and pays diminishing returns if it is not made subordinate to the truly musical purpose. Creative pianists showed how interpreters should first become sensitive to the musical language, before playing it. They were confident that purely technical expertise could not decipher the secrets of great music, and their example showed that a pianist needs inspiration, above all, to make new discoveries in his art and reach the top of his profession.

Marie Jaëll was the first to pose the question of whether piano techniques could be underpinned by scientific analysis. She remarked that most approaches downplay the obvious fact that music, product of human creation, is emotion-laden.

A skilled pianist has an intuitive inkling into the physics of the piano. But physicists and pianists champion conflicting views on piano action. According to scientists, the mechanical contact between the hammer and the key is broken before the hammer strikes the string; hence, the pianist has only a remote control of the impact that excites vibrations in the string. To them, it seems obvious that the player can influence only the loudness of single notes but not their quality. Nonetheless, they do admit that all musicians do not sound alike on the same piano.

Physicists forget that pianists are musicians, and that the piano is more a miracle of music than of physics. And pianists are convinced that they control the quality of sounds they produce on their chosen instrument. They are certain that they obtain delicate shadings in the character of the notes by applying different types of touch. Believing such a skill to be a decisive component of piano play, they learn to focus their keenest attention on just how they depress the keys. Marie Jaëll's entire pedagogy is based on her exact intuitions on the nature and structure of piano sounds produced by the touch.

No definitive scientific answer is in sight to justify this sense on the part of pianists. However, there are indications that they may be right. To explore and appreciate their viewpoint, we now turn to a detailed and careful analysis of "piano action."

The "actors" in order of appearance are the key, the levers, the damper, the hammer, the string, the bridges and the soundboard. "Piano action" stands for the complex of movements that occur from the moment a key is depressed till the moment the sound leaves the soundboard. At the areas of contact between the moving parts, one surface is covered with felt or leather to smother any backlash. What is within pianist's power is "the touch," that is, the gesture that pushes a key down, and unleashes the series of movements.

The keys can be pushed down, pressed or struck. They take some time to reach their bottom position on the key-bed. At the instant the pianist's finger touches a key, the levers spring to life, the damper is lifted off the string and, around 15 milliseconds later, fling the hammer from its rest position towards the string. Immediately after, the escapement mechanism intervenes to disconnect the key control from the hammer, which, carried by its momentum, swings freely for less than a millisecond during the final part of its travel before impacting the string. Soon after, the hammer withdraws; with the use of the double escapement mechanism, the key is let up only about a third of its travel. The damper returns to its initial position only when the finger is withdrawn from the key.

Thus the core of the action in the first instance consists of two contacts: the key touching the key-bed and the hammer-string impact. Between the two there is an unsuspected but strong link that has decisive artistic effects. At softer levels, key-bottom contact has a lag over the hammer-string contact: in *pianissimo* up to 35 ms after the string contact. At louder levels, it is ahead; in *fortissimo* the key reaches its bottom position nearly 5 milliseconds *before* the hammer strikes the string. At a certain dynamic level, i.e. at *mezzo forte*, the key reaches its bottom position just as the hammer strikes the string.

Typical maximum key velocities range from 0.1 milliseconds at *piano* to 0.6 milliseconds at *forte*. The final hammer velocities are much higher due to the force added by the levers, and range between approximately 1 and 5 milliseconds. There is no linear relationship between the motion of the key and the motion of the hammer. Thus the action will have very different effects at different dynamic levels. This phenomenon is also an essential component of the mechanical feedback from the instrument to the player. It contributes to the characteristic "feel" of the traditional piano action.

The link between the two contacts depends, probably on the way the key is pushed down, struck in *forte*, and pressed in *piano*. The time taken by the key to reach the bottom varies as a function of the dynamic level. This information is critical for the player's ability to perform the desired timing and synchronization of the notes. In order to achieve a soft dynamic level, therefore, the final hammer velocity must be low.

Thus the force of the player's touch controls the dynamic level. It also causes large changes in the timing patterns in the action. In grand piano action, the sensitive response enables the player to feel the pressure point at which the impulse is to be given. A touch at a soft dynamic level gives a late bottom contact in relation to the hammer-string contact. At a high dynamic level the pianist aims at a higher acceleration of the hammer that makes the touch resemble a blow than a push, superimposing strong oscillations on the key motion. In this case the hammer is accelerated heavily up to the bottom and the stop of the key is abrupt.

The hammer-string contact is another major determinant of the overtone content of the sound. The contact is not concentrated at a point, but is spread over as much as 5 or 10 millimeters along the string. The effective mass of the hammer increases only from about 12g in the bass to 6g in the treble. On the other hand, the string masses cover a much wider range, and in case of double and triple stringing, it is the total string mass for each note that counts.

Consequently, during the contact the hammer and the string are equal partners through much of the important middle range of the piano.

Given a fixed dynamic level, the duration of the hammer-string contact is determined by design factors such as the ratio between the mass of the hammer and the string, and the striking point along the string. It lasts a finite time, and changes slowly from about 4 milliseconds in bass to less than 1 millisecond in the highest treble. The force, communicated by the hammer to the string, varies in a complex way. As the contact duration decreases with rising level and the dynamic level grows from piano to forte, high-frequency overtones are given a boost. Consequently the bass notes, in contrast to the treble ones, will be richer in overtones.

The hammers bear a remarkable non-linear property. Normal felt hammers are soft and caress the string. When driven by higher impact velocities, they hit the string harder. Thus, a note in *forte* is not only an amplified version of the same note in *piano* but also contains many more high frequency overtones. It will therefore attain a different, even a "more brilliant" tone quality at *forte* than at *piano*.

Thus, a pianist's production of a weak or powerful sound depends on the degree of strength with which he presses the keys. Instinctively he obtains a sound that is not merely *piano* or *forte* but also with a gradation. The loudness and tone of a note are interdependent and are determined by the speed of the hammers.

The piano being a joint marvel of technology and art, it is normal that its sounds reflect their dual origin. Indeed, as the pianist touches a key, he sets in motion two sets of vibrations: first, those of the piano's mechanical parts; second, those of strings. Hence the final piano sound that emerges consists of two components: the vertical, called "thump" or "prompt" sound; and the horizontal, called "singing" or "after-sound." This fundamental distinction forms the core of Marie Jaëll's piano pedagogy.

It is easy to guess the origin of the prompt sound. The piano's key-bed, soundboard and iron frame are set in motion by an impact.

As a matter of fact, they are all excited at the moment a key hits the stop rail on the key frame. Under the shock, they all vibrate. Their contribution to the overall piano sound is the thump or prompt sound. It has a percussive trait. Not surprisingly, it has a certain resemblance to the noise in a blacksmith's shop. Such an evocative character, typical of the piano, is missing in the string component that follows. In fact, the singing string sound resembles the sound of a plucked string on other instruments. Once a musician learns to identify the two components, he easily distinguishes them in all piano tones.

The prompt component, at the onset of the note, plays a decisive role for the character of the piano tone. Undoubtedly, it depends on the performer's touch. It may be assumed to be characteristic of a pianist's way of playing. This component of the piano sound is so important that recognized piano manufacturers select the wood for the key-bed with great care, specifically in order to achieve the right resonance.

The touch plays a decisive role in the hammer's movement. Even when the dynamic level is kept constant, the hammer's movement gives rise to two components of oscillation, excited differently depending on the touch. The first is a slow backwash motion, more prominent in gentle touches, and the second is a "ripple" type of movement that is more prominent in the vigorous impulse-like types of touch. The pianist must be sensitive to such differences.

In addition, the hammer impact on the string generates a precursor in the motion of the bridge transmitted by longitudinal wave motion in the strings. This precursor may arrive at the bridge and excite the soundboard more than 10 milliseconds before the transversal string motion. A single string, vibrating at its fundamental frequency, goes in two directions. The prompt sound is simply related to the theoretical decay rate determined by way the string is coupled to the soundboard. The decay of the piano tone is complex and is of major importance in judging the tone quality

The "after sound," which gives the piano its perceived sustaining power, represents the "miracle." Thanks to the presence of more than one string for each piano note, and the consequent dynamic coupling that occurs among strings struck by the same hammer, the "after-sound" is reinforced and gives the tone its "singing quality."

The vertical polarization is the primary one excited by the hammer, and so begins its life at much higher amplitude than the horizontal one. However, since the bridge, which is attached to the soundboard, "gives" much more easily in the vertical than in the horizontal direction, the decay of the vertical mode is also much more rapid. As a result, the relatively slight amount of horizontal vibration becomes, after a while, dominant. The vibrations in the hammer may offer a possibility for the pianist to influence tone quality through touch, even though the mechanical contact between hammer and key is broken before string contact.

The human ear and brain are able to judge both loudness and sustaining power in a way that is not predictable. A sound is perceived as loud if it starts out loud, even if it then decays quickly. It is perceived as sustained if some of it is sustained even weakly. Thus a sound which starts out with a high but quickly decaying amplitude and which then having reached a rather low level switches to a much smaller rate of decay, so that there is a sustained but subdued after-sound, is perceived as being both loud and sustained. And that is precisely the miracle of the piano tone.

The action of the piano allows the pianist to control, by the force he applies, the speed at which the hammer strikes the strings — and, accordingly, the volume of each tone. A piano sound is pleasing and musical when the discordant frequencies produced by the hammer's vibrations are weak, and the harmonics of the string dominate. Thus it is desirable to reduce the prompt sound; although it is neither possible nor desirable to eliminate it completely. Its presence contributes to the unique sound of the piano. The pianist, however, can master the division of energy between forward motion and hammer vibration.

Even the way the fingers are withdrawn has an influence on the sound generated, since each note fades from the moment it begins. "When the hammer rebounds too quickly, the vibrating string brushes against it again several times as it falls back. Each of these supplementary contacts damages the sound. The hammer, so to speak, takes back the sound from the string. It extinguishes it; it stifles the sonority by preventing the vibrations from propagating."

There are different kinds of tonal beauty in the sound of the piano. Each pianist can develop a personal sonority that makes his or her work recognizable. It does not come from the way any individual sound is produced but from the balance of sound; and this balance can be vertical as well as horizontal.

The touch thus involves an infinitely complex amalgam of qualities, and certainly, the term is used in piano literature to denote several different aspects of piano technique. It may also indicate how the melody part can be lifted above an accompaniment or how certain notes in a chord can be emphasized.

With the piano instrument's latest technical advances, the technique came to be boiled down to training the fingers to initiate the right piano action in letting the hammers strike the strings. The essential ingredient of a successful technique became finger fluency. "Keep your hand still, Fräulein, don't make an omelet," Liszt told the American student Fay in 1873. Musical and dramatic effects were attained by phrasing; but few pianists could afford to devote sufficient time to work out the right touch.

Marie Jaëll's new piano technique consisted in teaching the fingers to adopt an action that sets the entire piano in motion. She had a well-developed instinct of observation. She had spent hours without end sitting beside Liszt, and she always wondered why he was so unique. She must have intuitively sensed the musical mechanics of the piano.

She also had an instinctive understanding of piano acoustics. Thus, starting from her particular awareness of Liszt's sonorities and attitude at the piano, she set out to research how to extract a sound that takes on life and recovers its primary purpose, which is to arouse people emotionally. Her attempts at a thorough overhaul of musical teaching in France made her a pioneer in the domain.

Led by her sharp sense of observation and her love for her art, Marie was one of the very first pianists to look seriously at piano pedagogy. The fight against the mechanistic approach, automatism, thoughtless and aberrant repetition, became her mission. She wanted to restore to the piano its proper function, and invited pianists to become authentic interpreters in the sole service of music.

Imagination, involvement and insight are the three qualities expected of someone who sets out to interpret a piece of music. Technique is essential, but as a means to an end. The secrets of great music are not easily deciphered. There are always new thoughts and new perceptions to be made. The secret of a pianist's success can be traced to his ability to obtain a constant gradation of emotion and a shading of tone, thanks to the subtlety of his timing. The beauty or vibrancy of sound he produces reflects his feeling of involvement and his comprehension of the substance of the music. Above all, a pianist must be filled with emotional and visceral or kinesthetic resonance if he is to play a piece so that he communicates a shared experience through tactile values.

The piano's golden age began in the 1870s. The piano had found its final form and was used for music at home and in the concert hall. A piano industry had come into being. The timing of Marie Jaëll's research could not have been more opportune.

3. THE TOUCH

WILL I HAVE MY SOUL AT MY FINGERTIPS?

The sound of the piano cast a spell on Marie Jaëll. It dawned on her that playing the piano was a creative activity spurred by enthusiasm, fire, imagination, and above all by the ability to feel, and to feel passionately.

The desire to regain the state of grace she had felt during certain concert evenings haunted her.

> I have to play this evening. Will I have my soul at my finger-tips? I want to reach the depths of souls...
> ...I did not play well... the beauty vanished like a dream...
> ...How can I make sure that the beauty does not flee like a dream?[73]

Such questions came to obsess her. Her reflections while still a child, looking at an engraving of Dante, underscore the force of her determination. She was forever tormented by the mysteries of

---

73. Jaëll, Marie, Journal (unpublished)

beauty and harmony, and felt an irresistible urge to unearth the laws of aesthetics.

Many pianists during the nineteenth century believed that it was Lady Chance smiling on them when they drew marvelous sounds from the instrument of their choice. Musicians attributed the ability to produce beautiful timbres to inborn talents that could not be acquired. Their prejudices led to piano teaching that was limited to trial and error procedures. Praise was heaped on students when they happened to produce the right sounds; when they failed, they were told luck had deserted them.

Such widespread views became anathema to Marie Jaëll. They were both irrational and ineffective, and were not backed by any physiological or physical justification. Her views are today confirmed by neuroscience. Now we know that "the ability to identify the absolute pitch of a tone without hearing it in the context of other notes is not a genetic predisposition but must be acquired through musical training."[74] All the same, it is true that talent for music has a certain heritable component. And training clearly "rewires" the musical brain.

Jaëll advanced what would seem to be unimpeachable proofs to defend her convictions. She used photography to analyze the hammer's action: it revealed that the nature of contact between the hammer and the string makes all the difference between a good and a bad timbre. On that basis, she realized, piano teaching must concentrate on how to influence the hammer-string impact.

True pedagogy is always an outflow of an overall vision. In her case it was guided by her mystical streak. She believed that music was a passport, as Berlioz boasted, to the divine and the transcendent. "Art is the strongest revelation given to the artist. It can only lead him there where all revelation leads a man of faith: towards God."[75]

---

74. Left in Music, *Nature*, August 13, 2001.

75. Jaëll, Marie, Journal (unpublished)

She never lost sight of that goal. All through the years, she came alive only when she was creating beautiful sounds that formed the platform for launching formless sounds, wafting her and her listeners to the world beyond the sensual and the material. Her entire pedagogy consists in the best exploitation of tangible resources to enter into the spiritual realm. She was also convinced that the ineffable mysteries of beauty and its creation could be the object of scientific investigation.

After sensing correctly the essentials of piano acoustics, she instinctively understood the global aesthetics of music. In her view, musical works are intentional products of the creative process as well as objects of intentional experiences for listeners.

Music is man-made sound and it is created to be listened to. With its atavistic links to dance, it is also bodily gesture. In that sense, a theory on how it is produced and how it must be heard needs to proceed from the principles of perception. In piano music, all sensory perceptions enter into the picture, and their synthesis takes place in the pianist's consciousness.

Marie Jaëll observed that only what is conscious can be perfected, and only what is consciously acquired can be transmitted. Thus at the core of her aesthetics is consciousness, and her entire pedagogy is built on the assumption that consciousness is primarily an ordinary biological phenomenon, for "no theory of aesthetics is likely to be complete, let alone profound, unless it is based on an understanding of the workings of the brain."[76]

The Romantic vision of humanity, in which she was raised, was the bedrock of her aesthetics. As an artist, she de-emphasized the idealism that was then in vogue, and that decreed body and mind to be separate. Such a sharp distinction between the physical reality described by science and the mental reality of the soul was responsible for disconnecting musical thought from fingering, and with that she could not agree. Indeed, it is impossible to build

---

76. Zeki, S. *Art and the Brain*, The Brain (ed) Edelman G.M. and Changeux J-P., (ed) 71-104

musical aesthetics on the philosophical dualism of conscious mind and unconscious body. Fortunately, new notions of psychology begin to be disseminated towards the end of the nineteenth century, and they called into question the Classicist vision of man. In her rejection of dualism in this context, Marie Jaëll was entirely modern. As Searle observes, "Many think they have a mind and body but that is not emphatically the current view among the professionals in Philosophy, Psychology, Artificial Intelligence, Neurobiology and Cognitive Science."[77]

Jaëll started with the existential link between emotion and music, and then between music and consciousness. Then she targeted consciousness, which controls the flow of perceptions and the multiple and dynamic relations among them. She was propelled by her deeply held conviction that aural, visual and tactile perceptions can realize their full potential in piano music.

Her aesthetics is also beholden to another Romantic tenet, one that emphasized the emotive power of art. "Without emotion, an artist cannot create." She believed that the sole aim of art is aesthetic bliss, and that a major feature of a work of art is its power to activate our inner chords. Unfortunately, sometimes musicology, the science of music, stays shy of emotion.

It was obvious to Jaëll that a beautiful sound moves us since, "in all art, emotion is the first condition of creation." Her research took its cue from the evidence of music's attraction for human beings, from its connection to the emotions. Truly, "music is stirring," and it has the power to disturb, arouse and inspire. It evokes full-blooded and strong reactions from listeners. There is meaning and emotion in music even though it is difficult to explain why music makes us feel the way it does. Surely, music encodes messages that are decodable by the human heart. It speaks the language of feeling and elicits feeling. It is the most basic of human creation. The deepest mystery is why music is so emotive.

---

77. Searle

Music is defined as patterns of sound varying in pitch and time and created for emotional, social and cultural purposes. How can one explain the sources of expressive power in music? In every culture, rhythmic sounds give listeners intense pleasure and unleash deeply felt emotions; rhythmic sounds can bond a community and dissipate tensions within it.

Music sounds the way emotions are felt, and that is what accounts for musical expressiveness. There is a unique bond joining music and human feelings. Music communicates feelings that cannot be expressed in words. It communicates nothing but formless events. Other symbolic systems, including language, lack music's power. Indeed, when humans talk about music they invariably have recourse to the language of emotions; and an emotion is a state of feeling, a state that bears specific relations to other states. In music, emotions are not induced by sounds alone but by their cognitive and experiential pointers.

The next problem consists in finding out how the form and contents of music and emotion match up to one another. Marie Jaëll felt certain that the profundity of music stems from its capacity to offer access to the divine. In her view, music gives access to the pure subject released from the world of objects, and obeys the laws of freedom alone. She claimed that her art seems to her only an eternal symbol of the infinite. Indeed, all art is an aesthetic experience whose basis is opaque and indeed should remain so. The wellsprings of artists' inspiration will remain ultimately a mystery.

Thus, in order to attain the first rung of musical art, one should become sensitive to sound's beauty. Only then does one have access to the sentiment of a more complex beauty, one that resides in the succession of notes and pitches. For emotions are not simple linear events. They are feedback processes. They come alive as the music's rhythm unfolds.

Marie Jaëll then moved on to another level of reflection. There is no art without thought. She did not subscribe to the idea that "the power of music lies in the way in which it works upon our feelings rather than in the way it works upon our thoughts." Art evokes emotion because it has a major component of significance. It is the intentional content of art that stirs people. She argued that the "more there is thought in art, the greater is that art."[78]

Emotions are pregnant with "intentionality." They are always caused by an idea and they cause an idea. Music also vibrates with intentionality. A musical piece, besides being a sequence of sounds, has a symbolic function and points to something beyond the sounds. This "intentional" property of music is intrinsic to it and indicates the state of emotions unleashed by it. Marie Jaëll's ambition was to relate such a key characteristic of music to conscious states.

Intentionality means movement and directedness. It is a conscious process aimed at a goal. It is a property of mental states and events and it defines their dynamics. It is not the same as consciousness but there is an overlap between the class of conscious states and the class of intentional mental states. The rendering of intentionality that informs a piece of art activates the whole apparatus of human consciousness. Ideas have to be understood and interpreted. Melody in music is permeated by intentionality and is always an interpretation as it comes in waves and loops.

Hence, Marie Jaëll sought to locate the nature and appeal of music by analyzing why sounds should be significant for consciousness. There is an ontological affinity between consciousness and sound. Both require time for their existence — but they do not require change. Both need duration and neither calls for extension.

In the case of piano music, the transfer of intentional content to consciousness and from the consciousness to the soundboard, so as to reach the emotions of listeners, passes through sensorial perceptions that are visual, aural and tactile. The pianist, before actually playing, has to feel the music with his whole body. His body must vibrate with the intentionality embodied in the musical piece he is going to perform. That is the splendor and challenge of the

---

78. *L'intelligence et le rythme*, p. 18

piano. In Marie Jaëll's vision, the true musical instrument is not the piano but the pianist.

Melody, harmony and rhythm induce a surge of emotions that mobilize man's entire being. Music making requires well-honed motor skills and relies on a high level of integration between auditory inputs and motion control. Neuro-science claims that the emotional response to music is processed in a set of structures widely distributed in the brain.

The pianist must become aware of his own body as the central point of all consciousness. The experience must become an inner, qualitative phenomenon. It is constituted by a flow of perceptions and by the relationships, both spatial and temporal, among them. In addition, there is a dynamic but constant synthesis of all such perceptions. It is governed by one unique personal perspective that is sustained throughout the performance. Such a sense of consciousness eludes neuroscientists' analysis, but it is central to a pianist as he plays the piano.

Any theory of consciousness has to account for the fact that all consciousness begins with the consciousness of the body. Our conscious perceptions are precisely experiences of the world that have an impact on our bodies. Our intentional actions consist typically in moving our bodies in order to have an impact on the world. Thus, from our earliest experiences of perceiving and acting, being conscious of our body is decisive for our consciousness. Movement, which implies both space and time, is once again at the core of such sensations.

The conscious experience of the body as an object in space and time is constructed in the mind. One of the most remarkable things about the brain is its capacity to form what neurobiologists today call the "body image." The brain's image of the body is at the basis of all perceptions. Consciousness of a sensation that is localized in any part of the body occurs in the brain. Indeed, the mind creates a constantly changing generalized idea of the body by relating the changes in bodily sensations from moment to moment. A sense of self is created by the relation between the body, more specifically the bodily sensation at any given moment, and the mind's image of the body. All of our conscious experiences are self referential in the sense that they are related to the experience of the self, which is the experience of the body image.

The phenomenon that people dance to music is a strong hint that music taps into the system of motion control. Muscle control embraces sequences of tension and release, and music recreates the motional and emotional components of movements. Indeed, music is the most basic form of human creation; and the nexus of music perception seems to lie closer to our ancient, primitive brain than to our recently evolved reasoning cortex. It certainly predates humans; it originated earlier than human language. Music and dance both take their meaning from and give meaning to time and space.

What accounts for consciousness is not the moments but the act of relating the moments of perception among themselves. The continuity of consciousness derives from the correspondence that the brain establishes from moment to moment with events in space and time. The vital ingredient in consciousness is self-awareness.

Marie Jaëll went on to analyze the relationship between the brain and touch. The human brain is not a general-purpose device. It has evolved in a series of adaptations to the requirements of sensation and action. The brain and the body co-evolved so that the brain could make the body function optimally. Since the skin is the largest organ of the body, and highly complex, touch plays a key role in the construction of "body images."

Unfortunately, touch has received less attention from researchers than it merits. Vision has typically dominated. Yet the fingers obtain information as to the inner workings of objects, whereas the eye remains fixed at the outer surfaces. Vision typically excels in discovering macro structures. Vision is perception at distance; in contrast, touch reports on the basis of direct contact with the object.

By its very nature, its range of perception is tiny, but its exploratory movements can cover the entire object. Its area of contact increases as the hand moves from one part of the object to another. Consequently the perception of the object is split up in space and time, at times partial but always sequential. The internal perceptions acquired via muscle activity and tendon articulations are supplemented by perceptions via the skin, and they all form one whole. Movement plays a central role in the use of touch; this explains why the most mobile regions are the most significant. In man, the hand constitutes the perceptive haptic system.

So, touch specializes in discerning microstructures. Indeed, the fingers surpass the eye in apprehending the thickness of papers, in detecting vibration, and other fine distinctions. It is well known that children, as soon as they learn to use their hands, are driven by a passion for touching. Whatever they see, they want to feel with their hands. Touch also means movement. Aristotle hailed the hand as "the instrument of instruments." Indeed, if we ponder what the human hand is capable of doing, we can only be filled with a sense of awe.

The dynamics of the relationship between the brain and the hand, the main organ of the sense of touch, forms the next rung in Marie Jaëll's pedagogy. The touch and the hand have influenced the brain. An intuitive appreciation of that linkage is reflected in the terms we use to describe cognition: so many are derived from the hand, like "comprehend," "handle" and "grasp." Scientists wonder if the human brain in its ascent created in the hand an organ commensurate with its creative ingenuity. Observations of children indicate that the demands of the brain spur the hand to ever greater improvement in its functioning. It is the brain that educates the hand. Kant rightly described a man's hand as his outer brain. The hand can be seen as the unique tool of the intellect, the bodily organ that best denotes the distinction between humans and beasts. It is wondrously engineered and is the prime visual site for the exercise of the art of memory. Touch and the hand have influenced language creation, and their contribution to piano music is equally fundamental.

Marie Jaëll went into ecstasies when she described the workings of the hand.

The wonderful tool, whose educative possibilities are still to be explored, this tool that is the hand. What a marvel, the Hand! We need our entire lives of contemplation to exhaust all its resources. The education of the hand opens up new perspectives before us. For it, I live; for its promotion I work.[79]

The repercussions of the development of tools, born of hand's ingenuity, are infinite, unforeseeable.

This instrument, given to us by nature, possesses inexhaustible and wonderful resources of variety and wealth.

On this point Marie Jaëll's thinking recalls Jung's ideas.

While studying the history of the human spirit [he writes], we are always struck again and again by the fact that the evolution of the mind goes hand in hand with the enlargement of consciousness, and that every step forward represents a painful and laborious acquisition. One would be tempted to say, what man hates most is to sacrifice a parcel of his unconsciousness. He has a deep-seated fear of the unknown.[80]

An English scientist of the time, concerned about the decline of manual training, sent out a cry of alarm: "The hand is going away," he would say, for he foresaw the possibility of the regression of the brain as a consequence of the regression of manual education.[81] But Marie added, "One could as well admit that this ill-adaptation of the hand for the accomplishment of more or less vulgar works is a happy sign because, as the old adaptations disappear, new adaptations that are destined to follow them will find favor." After all, there is no such thing as an ideal hand for a pianist.

One of the most powerful forms which helps train thought is that which stems from the education of the hand. The hand is

79. Marie Jaëll to H. Kiener
80. Quoted in Kiener
81. *Ibidem*

simultaneously an agent and interpreter in the development of the mind. The nature of our hand movements determines what we perceive and what we express. Touch involves ways of perceiving and representing reality that are beyond the powers of vision and audition. In addition, gestures have impact on thought. They highlight the overarching structure of discourse. In the production of piano music, a dialectics between gesture and sound is manifest.

Thus the pianist's hands are no longer just hands. They become symbols. His gestures are not just movements. They are symbols of action. They express the interpenetration of thought embedded in music. They are also tightly intertwined with music and indicate its meaning and finality. The two combine at a rhythmical pulse to provide a single presentation of meaning.

We must learn to regard the gestures and the sounds as different sides of a single underlying mental process. The hand and its movements are symbolic, and represent thought in action. The gestures reveal a new dimension of the mind, and provide differentiation of thought. They evoke the hidden images of the music. They also inject the pianist's personality into the music. Being part and parcel of a person's construction of thought, they disclose meaning in a given context. By actively influencing the music played, they carry it forward most expressively.[82]

Piano pedagogy must concentrate on the brain as a biological process so that it builds the right "body images" which move into action the instant the pianist takes over his instrument. This means consciously developing the movements of the hands. Years of practice shape the complex skills of a pianist's body, just as they shape the skills of professional dancers, and athletes. Of course, the human body is capable of an extraordinary range of movements. The brain develops control mechanisms that instantly activate the skilled movements of the hand when called for. "A musician will one day understand," Marie Jaëll once remarked, "that his mind is as

---

82. McNeill, D., *Hand and Mind, What Gestures Reveal about Thought*, University of Chicago Press, 1992

much in his hand as in his brain, and that the most reliable and the most personal educator he has is his hand."[83] "If you do not awaken the eyes that are in your hand," she added, "you will not achieve anything worthwhile."

The huge repertoire of movements that a pianist masters is stored in the memory. Memory and consciousness are intimately related, and one cannot exist without the other; memory is not a passive storehouse of information. It is a continuing activity of the brain that actively processes and re-categorizes the inputs. Motions spring to consciousness from the dynamic interrelations of the past, the present and the "body image."

The processes of the "unconscious," which means memory, are not ordered in time. The relation to time is linked to the workings of consciousness; consciousness unfolds in time. The unity of consciousness guarantees that all forms of our conscious life, including bodily sensations, visual perceptions and thinking, are unified into a single conscious field.

Marie Jaëll marvelously intuited that intentionality means movement with a goal. This is the reason why mental representations, according to her, take such an importance in musical performance. As she observed,

> To give expression by a movement of the least dimension is to enhance one's consciousness of it, and to intensify it. The most minute, the most subtle sensations (motive, tactile, and auditory) require the greatest mental effort. The operations of the mind are invisible, elusive and infinitely delicate but we know how powerful are their effects. Man has enveloped his greatest strength in his thought.[84]
> ...If movement is the most immediate factor of thought, how can it be desecrated by automatism and thoughtlessness?[85]

---

83. Jaëll, Marie, Notebooks (unpublished)

84. Jaëll, Marie. *L'intelligence et le Rythme*

85. Jaëll, Marie. *Musique et psychophysiologie.*

Clearly, explicit knowledge is intimately linked to consciousness. Indeed, it is difficult to acquire knowledge in an unconscious way. Therefore, argued Marie Jaëll, why not make efforts to awaken all these sensations to consciousness rather than waiting for them to come into play by chance alone? By making a more conscious effort to trigger them, she sought to help everyone realize the beauty of the piano. To understand the mechanisms of how playing piano stirs the emotions and how artistic beauty is created became her passion.

Underlying the succession of movements there is a truer and more essential character, which must be appreciated intellectually by the artist and must be attentively grasped, and given a more lasting impression. Music and the hand have a changing relationship in deep time. Their synthesis is maintained on the basis of rhythm. Fingering, hand movements and music form elements of a single integrated process. The hand moves along with the rhythmic pulsation of speech. Its gestures convey meanings through a palpable space. They are symbols that point to something beyond the material. They transform thought into image and music.

In this context, what is called "banging" in terms of piano playing simply means playing the notes of a chord all equally loud, with no attempt to adjust the individual notes within a chord and manage the way they resonate. It is the artful balancing of the different notes within chords that produces a sound that is singing, expressive.

Marie Jaëll abhorred the view that the mind was entirely confined to the brain. In her view, the thought to be communicated triggers a train of events throughout the nervous system. It may be localized in the fingertips, in the nerve endings. In response, the pressure of the fingertips unleashes a sequence of neuron firings that begin at the sensory receptors in our skin, and make their way back to the brain. Thus piano pedagogy must teach the pianist how to control both the pressure of his fingertips on the keys and the speed of his movements.

There is a third dimension to consciousness, and that is the social. Humans form communities that exist within a web of meaning. This web, also referred to as culture, is what complements and completes the internal attributes of consciousness. Symbolic thinking is a form of consciousness that extends beyond the here and now to a contemplation of the past and the future, and a perception of the world within and beyond one individual. Communicating through abstract symbols is the foundation of all creativity in art, music and language. It is a paradox that consciousness, which is self-referential, is also the condition that makes it possible for anybody to be of importance to anybody.

Thus piano music is communion between the pianist and the piano, and between the pianist and the listeners. By his touch the pianist brings the piano to life. He communicates with his listeners through sounds, facial expressions and bodily movements. His performance recalls the primitive connection of music with dance. In sum, piano music is a kind of liturgy that transports all the participants to the divine.

Jaëll's remarks on Rubinstein's performances fully illustrate the basic principles of her pedagogy.

> The mechanical chaos he realizes on the keyboard with his ten fingers is an inspired performance. But he does not produce more music than the wind when it makes the leaves of a tree quiver, the water in a stream as it glides over the stones, the cascades as they plunge into the depths, because in these three different manifestations the successive movements originate from a harmonious exchange of forces. If the musical spirit is to be manifested by materially determined actions that are transmitted to the fingers, the esoteric nature of musical language will cease to exist. The fingers at the keyboard will merely find movements that transmit expressions just as writing transmits thought.

Thus, the three main axes around which she structures her pedagogy are: first, movement is a prop to thought; second, thought controls movement; third, sensation awakens and feeds thought.

From there, she turns to a practical analysis of movements as symbols of action in space and their relation in piano play. The Romantics believed that musical sounds were symbols and argued that the continuity with which lines in space or sounds in time follow each other is the natural symbol of the inner consistency of the mind and the moral connection between action and emotion. Jaëll's objective was to develop a musical pedagogy to help pianists realize the Romantic dream.

BEFORE PLAYING THE MUSIC, BE THE MUSIC

The musicologist Schenker notes that music, built on a foundation of harmony, is radically new. The traditional musical forms were architectural and symmetrical around a center. They recalled the circle, the symbol of being-in-itself, where time stands still. By contrast the new music recreated time-as-an-arrow, flying towards a target. It is a dynamic flow of infinite relationships among the overtones of a single sound. Its forms carry directedness and forward motion, and create the experience of time as a process. Such a change in musical structure inspired Marie Jaëll's conception of music as movement and direction, as path and goal. Her metaphor for music was a moving circular line, an infinite line that is a circle driven by an endless chain of loops.

To appreciate the joys of such a marvel, a novel pedagogy is required. Led by her spiritual vision of art, she explained successively how a pianist should bring to life the harmony, rhythm and melody that inform a piece of music. Her novel technique, which she called "the touch," targets the emotion-laden thought content underlying the music. Her one purpose was to enable the pianist to learn how to be an instrument of music, and exploit to the full the fundamental property of the piano to grandly vary the effects of harmonies by balancing the sound in different ways.

Her method, which superficially appears to involve the fingers alone, becomes a probing of the musical brain. It appeals to the laws followed by the cerebral cortex in fusing the aural, visual and tactile sensations activated by the sounds. Her discoveries send her into raptures, and she exclaims, "it is wonderful to feel that one has let one's soul pass through the ivory keys. It is wonderful to hear it vibrate and to feel that it makes other beings vibrate." Truly, she transforms her enquiry into an intellectual science of sensations unleashed by music that the keyboard helps resonate.

Her theory takes off from the correlation between movements at and within the piano that take place in milliseconds and the corresponding brain processes that occur at the level of neurons. A pianist produces a wide range of nuances of musical expression by activating his instrument's 88 keys, none of which travels a distance longer than one centimeter. The consequent rhythms with their subtle and fleeting transformations fall beyond the limit where (generally speaking) the pianist's conscious perceptions stop. Such phenomena form the raw material for her experimental analysis in piano instruction. The objective of her pedagogy is to help a pianist streamline his micro-conscious level perceptions.

The decisive quality of piano music depends on the pianist's ability to produce pure sounds, defined by their absolute pitch, the foundation stone of harmony. Thus, the ability to name a solitary tone without any other tones by way of reference is a prized musical talent and a scientific mystery. There is a lively debate as to whether its instant recognition depends more on a genetic predisposition that provides greater musical awareness, or early experience, i.e., music lessons. Present-day studies confirm Marie Jaëll's intuition that such a trait can be acquired through childhood training. However, it is not clear that training alone can create great musicians.

Outwardly, the piano action commences at the moment the pianist's fingertips touch the keys. The keyboard is a highly elaborate and complex mechanical interface. The quality of the pianist's playing depends in large part on the manner in which he accelerates the keys, and communicates force to them, thus controlling the velocity and timing of the hammers impacting the strings. He can vary such qualities by changing the direction of his fingertips, for instance. From a physicist's viewpoint, the average downward acceleration of the key determines the loudness and volume of a note.

In normal playing, the fingers bend slightly as they depress the keys. To begin with, fingertip's motion can be split into two components. If it is almost vertical, a loud sound is produced; if it is almost horizontal, a soft sound results. When a key is hit from above, it will jar the hammer into strong vibrations and most of the energy will go into those vibrations, yielding a strong but quickly vanishing thump sound. On the other hand, if the fast-moving fingers just glide smoothly over the keys and depress them gently, almost all the energy is transformed into a long-lasting "singing" sound. In this case the dissonant frequencies produced by the hammer will be minimal. When a difference between two equally loud piano tones is perceived, it can be traced to the way the keys are activated, and hence to the different noise components involved in the keystroke The finger-key noise component giving the prompt sound is audible when the key is struck and absent when it is pressed down.

Is that all there is to the touch? What, then, does it mean when we say "touch" the piano? What meaning can that simple word have for the pianist, and where will it lead him in his musical quest? The physical contact between the finger and the key is established at the fleshy part of the fingertip, the hand's most sensitive and receptive parts. The fingertips are tightly packed with cataneous receptors and their free nerve endings are fine sensory fibrils. The pressure of fingers on keys launches a sequence of neuron firings that take off at the sensory receptors in the skin and end in the brain. The piano action, as it releases the flow of sounds, sends instant messages back to the brain. The fingertip pulps give and receive at the same time. They transmit energy to the keys and receive at the same time mental feedback. One could say that, with piano music, the fingers are but masons who build, and the supreme architect who oversees is the brain.

Marie Jaëll realized that the particular way in which the keyboard is touched has a decisive impact on the sound's timbre and, consequently, on the quality of musical expression. A mechanistic approach to playing the piano was anathema to her (as to the majority of pianists of her epoch). Most people, as they master the physicality of their instrument, lose the sense of their instrument. What is worse, they lose the sense of what they are and of what music is.

> Imagine a tempest breaks out [she observed], and there are three different persons present. The first one hears only the howl-ing of the wind; the second one only suffers the violent fluttering of the clothes he wears; and the last one only feels the raging wind lashing at his face...These three sensations give a complete repre-sentation of the tempest's nature only when one and the same per-son experiences them. It is exactly the same situation for the realization of musical art; it is through the development of our three main senses of touching, hearing and seeing that we reach a true understanding of music. Great artists naturally sense such a correlation, and exploit it unconsciously. This is the reason for their superiority.[86]

In her view, touch involved a maze of possible sensations all operating together and affecting each other; and this complexity of interrelations helped music realize Romanticism's dream of speaking heart to heart. In the first instance, however, it suggests the physical contact between the pianist and the piano. She calls therefore called on pianists to master all the complex series of body movements that transmit energy from the keys to the hammers and the strings. To her, the physical gestures that are part of piano playing are but the visible expressions of the brain activity that commands the relationships among the visual, aural and tactile sensations.

She had an intuitive feel for the intricate interplay between the piano's dynamics and the pianist's artistry. She viewed it as a

---

86. Quoted in Kiener

continuous and sustained exchange of actions and reactions, of give and take. The fingers are in contact with the keyboard, and the sensation of touch, from the moment the fingertips press the keys until their withdrawal, unleashes a chain of other tactile, aural and visual reactions. All such sensations create a symbiotic union between the pianist and his piano. But he is conscious only of a small number of them.

Delacroix likened the modern painter to a performer exploiting his palette like a keyboard. To Marie Jaëll, the first joint of a pianist's finger is the palette, with all its rich potential for creating infinite variations of touch. The first joint enables him to vary the character of timbres in the same way that a painter can mix an infinite range of shades and hues, before he even approaches the canvas. The Romantics hailed pianists as the painters of sounds.

For the pianist, as for the painter, a faulty method of fingering — whether of the keyboard or the brush — can lead a lack of harmony in that touch. When an artist's touch fails to fall in line with the idea animating his art, he is unable to transmit the right images in sounds or in colors.

The fingers alone, when energized by the idea underlying the music, can outdo all arm action to produce loud sounds. Their force gains added strength as their movements mirror and simulate the musical thought processes. Liszt, more than anyone else, was aware of this transformation. People tended to attribute his spectacular style to the visible articulation of his finger movements, when it was in fact an outcome of the hidden, complex processes elaborated in his brain. He was deeply unhappy that his admirers spoke of his "magic fingers" and had no inkling of the mental powers he drew on while he was at the piano.

Hence, it seemed, the foremost skill a pianist should acquire is the intuitive use of his sense of touch. And, Marie Jaëll was certain that it could be cultivated by conscious training. From physiologists she learned the decisive role of tactile perception in the formation of brain images and in the acquisition of manual skills, and that confirmed her intuition.

Thus, in her training, she asked pianists to use their hands in movement, as antenna, and not as "paws." Two goals — to awaken the hand and to endow it with life — become the fundamentals of her teaching. Then she proceeded to elaborate the premises of her pedagogy. She argued that with our hands we take and give, and with our sense of the touch we identify an object, recognize a texture and feel a tissue, and we measure and compare things. As an aside, she remarked that our hands adjust their rhythm as we offer a present to a friend and translate unknowingly what is in the back of our mind. Their movements get a fillip when we give with a good heart, but they slow down to express regret.

Thus, Marie Jaëll enjoined her pupils to work their fingers regularly and build up their strength. She emphasized that hands are capable of acquiring extraordinary power and of conveying the maximum intensity of harmonious sensations. In cajoling terms, she explained that those who wish to play piano have no right to leave their precious hands, which are responsible for fashioning brain images, uneducated.

Her observations are once again backed by modern neuroscience, which highlights the close connection between consciousness and motor control. To acquire expertise in physical movements, one must engage in deliberate exercises. Of course, conscious practice is a unique form of activity that demands goal-oriented and concentrated effort in order to hone and improve specific mental and physical skills.[87]

Catherine Pozzi exclaimed, as she worked with Marie Jaëll:

> What a beautiful compass to measure the universe you have given me. I feel my hands did not experience the music until this true harmonization, this music made flesh, was acquired. It seems to me that I can go far along this path. I am scared at the idea of sensing the resonance that I feel between my fingers.[88]

87. Rossano, M.J., "Expertise and the Evolution of Consciousness," *Cognition* October 2003, 207-236

88. C. Pozzi's letter to M. Jaëll

The art of touch filled Marie with awe. She systematized the principles into a science in order to put it within everyone's reach. She believed that "the touch" would be a powerful method to help people accede to authentic musical expression, and so she focused her full attention on the training and refinement of the hand's movements. She enjoined pianists to pay attention to the physiology of their bodies and especially of their hands, so that they might become conscious of the circles of enchantment spinning around them. Once a pianist is aware of them, he can start mastering them.

To test her method, Marie launched what she called "the new system of piano teaching." She urged her students to devote their fullest attention to consciously acquiring tactile sensitivity, and to refine it. Those who followed her instructions soon succeeded in radically transforming their poor sonorities. She gave public recitals in the *Salle Pleyel* with her pupils. Their performances were a far cry from the mechanistic noise produced by other children of the same age. The wonderful sounds and harmonies of their music enchanted the public. Such a spectacular success flowed from her touch method that insisted on intelligent rather than mechanical acquisition of skills.

Charles Lamoureux (1834-1899), who was present at most of her auditions, was full of enthusiasm. A violinist of distinction, he was responsible for popularizing classical music in France. He asked Marie to let her pupils perform at his Thursday morning sessions. She replied with a firm no, for, she said, she had to confirm the results she had obtained; and she returned to her research.

She was not one to rest on her laurels, nor to offhandedly attribute her successes to her deep intuitions as an artist. She conjectured that a scientific analysis of touch would have to be made. She studied Darwin, Bain, Paulhan, Marey, Leibnitz, Gratiolet, and Binet in order to get a better grasp of human physiology and psychology. She paid particular attention to the theories of Féré and Helmoltz, on visual and aural perceptions, as they became known throughout Europe between 1850 and 1890.

And, soon enough, in 1893, her first book appeared: *Touch, New Elementary Principles for Piano Teaching*. In the book's introduction she says,

> All piano teaching must start by a rational study of touch. It will consider how the notes, far from following each other like the letters of an alphabet, form groups... The pianistic technique consists in learning to mobilize the multiple sensorial resources we have at our disposal to express a musical text.

In other terms, already from the start, the new method gives music the importance of its language, and not the other way.

Her decisive contribution to the touch technique was her analysis of what she calls the "geometry of sensations." The pianist, as he takes the measure of an interval between his fingers, provokes in them transversal vibrations that are related to precise aural sensations. More important, his tactile sensations spread out along linear paths traced by the nerve endings at his fingertips. As he plays a piece of music, his hands feel that all their fingers are inter-linked by invisible and inelastic threads through all the planes in space. A hand, made sensitive, conscious, open to the space, vibrates in contact with the space and becomes conscious of its relationship with it. It becomes a universe of sensations.

According to Chopin, each finger has fundamentally a unique character.[89] He urged pianists to exploit the specific properties of each finger in order to obtain subtle gradations of color inflections of phrasing. In his view, the delicate passages of a piece of music ought to be played by the weakest fingers, and lyrical melodies, with more emphatic notes of singing, should be reserved for the stronger fingers — often to one finger alone.

Marie Jaëll provided a rational underpinning to Chopin's intuitions. She claimed that every finger is gifted with a unique feel, so it must be treated as an independent actor, capable of creating myriad sensations. The angle and direction of its strike can impart

---

89. Rosen, C. "The Chopin Touch," *The New York Review of Books*, May 28, 1987 :9-13

delicate and differentiated nuances to a sound's timbres. A pianist as he trains his hand for the touch makes sure that each finger cultivates a distinct personality of its own.

Next, she observed that fingertip sensations are spread across linear pathways formed by the touch organs. Each of the multitude of tiny nerve endings forming such lines serves a distinct function and is endowed with a specific transmission speed. Consequently, each finger has a unique touch that is a synthesis of the multiple feels proper to its least surface area. The minutest part of the pulp at which the contact with the key is localized contributes decisively to sound production. To exploit such a rich resource, the pianist must learn to irrigate the sensory apparatus with musical thought along the orientation of embedded linear paths.

Paying attention to fingers one by one is related to the process called "the dissociation of fingers." This involves a deliberate separation of fingers in order to increase their individual capacity to spread out, and thus broaden the spaces between them. As the dissociation of the fingers is refined, the pianist experiences invisible threads linking tactile sensations through empty spaces. In this way, the silent music diffusing through the fingers and the tactile sensations join the auditory sensations to express harmony. Once more, such a mastery of the intermediary spaces is the outcome of a unique way of thinking. But the movements, dissociated and executed by the fingers, become artistic only if their image pre-exists in the brain.

Thus, while the fingers press the keys, relatively minimal changes in the linear orientation of the pulp can provoke decisive changes in muscular sensations. The last four fingers have pulp regions that are most sensitive to the least dimension. That is, the touch of the index finger enables us to perceive the most reduced dimension while the least sensitive, the fifth finger, specializes in the perception of bigger dimensions.

While mastering the dissociation of fingers, the pianist must learn how the fingers can act together. When the key is struck with the top joints of the thumb and the index finger combined, a change in the rhythm of musical thought occurs instantly and the ears hear a different timbre. The brain images can be so developed that the pianist's two hands, without being together, give the impression of being superposed in such a way as to form just one. Thus one can have a simple representation of each hand and, at the same time, a unified representation of both the hands. Then the pianist's thought seems to act directly on his left hand and indirectly, through his left hand, on his right hand. Out of such indirect action will emerge the most intense artistic stimulation.

The sensations flicker differently in the different fingers of each hand and the artistic nature of the music is revealed only under the mutual influence of the sensations of the five fingers of the left hand on the sensations of the five fingers of the right hand. In fact, there is more to this idea, for the pianist's brain functions as if it perceives twenty-five fingers in each hand, and the indirect influence exercised by the twenty phantom fingers coincides with the harmonics of the sounds emitted. In this way the multiple fingers, real and phantom, are the brain's keyboard and form the counterpart of the piano's keyboard. During the simultaneous movements of different fingers, one and the same cohesion must exist and must be the basis of the intellectuality of the play.

To Marie Jaëll, Liszt was the paragon of pianists. He excelled in the dissociation of fingers that reflected the transcendent brain activity of his playing. He had a distinct brain-image for each of his finger movements and mastered the exact proportionality for their combination. From watching him play, she learned that the maximum fertilization of musical thought goes hand in hand with maximum transparence of sounds. The pre-existing brain images contain the rhythmic speed of musical phrases and drive the fingers to transmit it to the keyboard.

The pianist's brain transforms the musical phrase into a rhythmic movement. During such a process it becomes fertile and communicates the harmonies of the rhythm to the fingers. He views his body, and even the space, filled with his music, only in relation to the signals acquired by his tactile sensations and to the force imparted by those signals.

In the pianist's brain, since his early infancy, myriads and myriads of images of the outside world are stored — images of the world in relation to himself. They constitute his unconscious, or memory, which is not just a passive receptacle but an active process of re-categorizing. As he is driven by the musical idea, his brain picks up the appropriate finger movement to realize it in sounds. Thus, it may not be completely true to say that the fingers have a reason of their own, that "reason" knows not of. Improvisation is not exactly unconscious, but it is clear that the fingers develop a partially independent logic that is then ratified by the mind. Only then does interpretation function very much like improvisation. What looks like an instinctive muscular reaction of the body is, in fact, the outcome of a reasoned and planned program.

Marie Jaëll's results unlocked new worlds both for pupils and teachers. Her methods call on both to concentrate on an intelligent training of their hands. They help a pupil increase his awareness of the world of possibilities of his hands, to learn the precision of his touch, and to develop his tactile and aural senses, all in order to create a sound that is pure, exact, and harmonious and to sculpture the sonorous matter. They oblige him to start by first immersing himself into the depth of the music he will play. Then he himself becomes a creator, since he directs and induces the texture of sounds, and links them among themselves as if he is recounting a story in another language. A young child, as he makes progress in piano music, already marvels at his ability to bring to life beautiful sounds with the pressure of his fingers on the keys, and loft them across space towards a paradise of formless sounds. From the very first lesson the notions of beauty and listening are instilled in him. With his touch the young pupil learns to create a timbre that reflects him. Once more, the findings of modern neurobiology give scientific grounding to Marie Jaëll's intuitions. They highlight that perceptual cognition, especially with respect to the bodily spatial dimension, arises in early infancy.

In the new pedagogy, freedom of fingers, suppleness of movements, and rapidity of sound emission form the fundamental principles of a good touch.

> As soon as one succeeds in preventing the pupil from stiffening his hands and fingers as he plays, he already has a nice touch at his command. For it is the immobility in which one maintains the finger after pushing the key that, above all, gives rise to the stiffness. As one draws from the instrument a vibrant and expressive sound, one is struck by what a touch can do as it impresses on the key a little glide which is nothing else but the principle of suppleness of touch.

Albert Schweitzer, her pupil at the time, translated her book into German. "I owe so much to this inspired woman," he remembered later. "While working under her guidance I completely transformed my hand. Thanks to rational study, which took a little time, I have become a better master of my fingers. My play at the piano also gained from it." And he added, "The fundamental ideas of Marie Jaëll's method are among the most profound that have been formulated on the art of touch."

In 1896, Marie Jaëll published her first book meant for the general public: *Music and Psychophysiology*. It was immediately translated into German and Spanish, and brought to her a flood of students from Paris as well from America, England and Holland. She wrote to inform one of her friends:

> I have finished my new book.... I was buried in it, so much so that when spring came, I thought I had slept all through winter. But those who will read it ought not to fall asleep if they have any feeling for what is new. Are you a Physiologist? If not, I hope you will be one in the future for it would be a pity if this brilliant science did not light your path one day. You think I am gone crazy. Nenni, I only possess highly developed senses. You will grasp everything that I say when you have read my book. Thanks to the movements that I have found by myself, I can teach everyone to realize beauty with the piano. What bliss! You ask me what people in Paris think of my book. Oh! Nothing at all. Three people

liked it: Jeanne Bosch, a pupil; Camille Saint-Saëns, an artist; and Charles Féré, a scientist.

And like it they did. Jeanne Bosch van's-Gravemoer put all her intelligence, energy, and even her wealth at her teacher's disposal. She was fully convinced that the new approach to the instrument was right. Regrettably, an incompatibility of character between the two led to their separation a few years later.

Camille Saint-Saëns was full of praise for the book. After several years of silence, he wrote to her, "I could only half open your book. The rays that radiated from it dazzled me. Its form and content both seem to me equally admirable. One cannot think or say better, express more clearly things that are more instructive and judicious, more beautiful and true. This little book will follow me everywhere."

Marie Jaëll's book also caught the attention of Charles Féré, distinguished physiologist and the Head Doctor at the Hospice of Bicêtre. Gifted with a remarkable sense of observation, he was renowned for his work on the hand and its movements. He enjoyed a great reputation in scientific circles. As a contemporary article noted, "Doctor Féré, with a spirit of boundless energy, balanced, stubborn, and having an extraordinary capacity for work, has published a series of books and countless articles in the Scientific Reviews. His work represents a formidable accumulation of facts examined under all their forms, presented with sincerity, and shorn of all metaphysical concerns. In all his works we find new facts, clever ideas, sometimes bold, but always measured, and stamped with common sense." Féré was preparing to publish a volume on *The Hand*, his teacher Broca having exhorted his students that the exploration of the mechanism of the hand ought to be the goal of future research.

Féré believed that "psychologists devote too little attention to studying the hand. The hand is simultaneously an agent and an interpreter in the development of the mind. It deserves more attention from physiologists and psychologists." He found the echoes of his work in Marie Jaëll's; and in her book she explicitly refers to his findings.

Fascinated by Marie Jaëll's ideas, Féré went to see her and proposed they work together. She accepted, and they began a period of intense collaboration that would last till 1907, the year he passed away.

Their meeting marked the beginning of a remarkable collaboration. Both shared the same passion for the study of the links that bind the hand to the brain, of the importance of the consciousness of movements, and the physiology of touch. In her work Marie sought to shed light on the relations between man and art, and Féré brought to her all the rigor of his knowledge and his scientific methods. Both were relentless workers, and daring in matters of research. They were kindred spirits, and Marie found in him "the sovereign moral support" about which Edouard Schuré had spoken in his correspondence to her.

In a letter written years later to one of her pupils, Marie recalled their joint work.

> Between 1897 and 1907, I was not working alone, Doctor Féré communicated to me all his research results as I communicated mine to him. It was at 14 *rue Tournon* that he let me make repeated fingerprints of the same tuning.... I continued the work with unflagging interest until I discovered the results that you know...
>
> I looked for exact movements, and thanks to these movements I found the harmony of touch, musical memory, the perfecting of the ear, all those faculties that seem dormant in all of us. My research was continually monitored by experiments in Doctor Féré's laboratory at Bicêtre.

Marie Jaëll and Charles Féré worked together to analyze the myriad sensations that are centered in the hand. Their objective was to obtain scientific knowledge of hand movements in order to become more aware of them, to bring them into the conscious realm where they can be used intentionally. They invented experiments to unearth the connections among auditory processes, hand movements and brain-images. Their results led to the following suggestions.

The pianist should not concentrate on mastering musical scales automatically. He is invited to [practice scales in order] to become conscious of his sense of touch — which is quite often anaesthetized; to refine the sensation of the grip, the sensation of the spaces between the fingers, the sensation of opening the entire palm of the hand, of all that links us to the world and others.

Then his music becomes palpable, and the interpreter resembles a sculptor, opening wide his hands through the sonorous sound in order to give. The artist's gift is no longer a present from heaven that makes him talented, as they say; it is rather his ability to know how to give others this gift from heaven.[90]

Marie Jaëll wanted to ban automatic movements from piano learning. She structured her lessons around the cultivation of consciousness. The basic principle of her teaching was, "Know thyself!" To her, conscious work was priceless because it developed intelligence. In fact, consciousness only exists when it is experienced as such, and the consciousness and the experience of consciousness are the same thing. Only what is acquired by a conscious effort can be transmitted, since it is deeply experienced. And, to transmit is precisely what pedagogy is about.

She argued that within our unconscious all our possibilities are locked up, the lowest as well as the highest. Thought has the task of subjecting our instincts and intuitions to lucidity in order that the worlds buried in our inner depths are awakened, enter into action and take form in the physical world. Some cognitive scientists claim that we unconsciously follow the rules; Marie Jaëll argued that an unconscious rule has to have the kind of content that can be consciously understood, interpreted, followed or violated.

She subscribed unconditionally to the view that "all acts of becoming conscious are creative acts." To her the first conscious act of a pianist consists in his becoming aware of his body, of his hands

---

90. Jaëll, Marie, collectif Symétrie, édition de musique et services aux musiciens.

and of his perceptions. Concentrating on that will let his body vibrate with the music he is going to play. His being then becomes the actual musical instrument to which the piano serves as a mirror and transforms his sensorial combinations, failed or true, into bad or good music. "Your body is a musical instrument. You must succeed in tuning this instrument which is you, your intelligence, all your structure, your hand."[91] From this viewpoint, piano playing becomes a creative process that bonds the pianist to his piano in a tight embrace.

From this point on, Marie's life continued without major outside events intervening. She wrote a series of books that described the fruits of her research. She taught and formed close ties with her pupils. She was not an ordinary professor, and she marked with her stamp all those worked with her.

Among them was Catherine Pozzi, that exemplar of aristocratic and bourgeois life in *fin de siècle* Paris, who speaks at length in her diary of her meeting with Marie Jaëll. Born in 1882, she was already sent to a piano teacher in 1885, a teacher who, it was said, was a genius — but overbearing. Of course, it was Marie Jaëll. Early in her adolescence, Catherine would go once a week to *rue de Tournon*. Later on, the two formed a team. As we read her diary, we realize how important her meetings with Marie Jaëll were, at every stage in her life. She wrote,

> Before [I can go ahead with this], I must re-invent myself...as one who is not afraid of being alone.
> ...I went to the closest thing: my work with Jaëll.
> ...Jaëll was there. Those who would later work with her in the spirit of the most beautiful of human endeavors were the only ones who could understand that it was enough for me to follow her unique wisdom, her discipline, for a few months, and all the bandages with which I was mummified fell apart, rotten, broken... Power, genius: you have made me...[92]

---

91. Jaëll, Marie. Journal (unpublished)

92. Pozzi C., *Journal*, Ramsay

Even so, Marie was terribly demanding, and at times impatient. Her pupil found it difficult to follow her, but she was not disheartened for she loved music with an instinctive and passionate love, and recognized an extraordinary and exceptional character in the personality of her professor.

Working with Marie was a source of comfort and enrichment to Pozzi. The new method of touch helped her learn and master musical expression, by degrees. Above all, in contact with her teacher, she seemed to fulfill her own personality. The two exchanged countless letters during their lives. Catherine often spoke of her aspirations, pains, joys, worries, and Marie always had the intuition to suggest the right answer, and to give support. Marie was a source of indefinable radiance that only exceptional personalities exude, as her pupils' letters bear witness.

Catherine Pozzi wrote to her:

> Dear Madame, I often think of you. You seem to me — I'll just say it — like my destiny itself. I have often believed obscurely in fate, although my scientific environment turned me away from it... Socrates used to say that virtue is learned, and having once possessed it, one cannot lose it. Following your method I have become Socratic. I do not accept that one can, after having practiced it, run after something else. Willingly, I would decide with Socrates that, in that case, one never did possess it. Once upon a time, I studied Philosophy, and with passion. Not for a diploma, but only to find a reason to live. I have been driven from ecstasy into despair, then into indifference. Ever since I have been working my hand regularly, the eyes of my intelligence are opened; I have entered into certainty. There is a complete ethic hidden in your work; it is the best and the truest of my life. What a beautiful compass you have given me to measure the universe! It can be applied to everything.

Marie's method filled the people around her with enthusiasm because it contains the essential elements that move a human being deep in his humanity. They came to realize that the hand's sensitivity opens up an entire new world of emotions and perfect expression. Truly, to touch is also to be touched.

Marie Jaëll continued her research untiringly, supported by Charles Féré. With him she co-authored several articles in scientific journals. She published her second book in 1897: *The Mechanism of Touch: The Study of the Piano through Experimental Analysis of Tactile Sensitivity.* This is really a scientific work for a musician; it shows how advanced she was in conducting rigorous experiments in order to test her intuitions.

"Every time there is an improvement of sonority in the performance of a work, an analysis of fingerprints shows that it corresponds to better contacts."[93] Seeking to understand how a pianist plays by studying his fingerprints was certainly a novel approach to the subject; Marie pursued that and many other paths.

In this book she describes her experiments in minute detail, along with the conclusions she draws from them concerning the diverse regions of the fingertip of each finger and their relationship with sonority. For long years she gave herself to research, with infinite patience, comparing the fingerprints of different pianists. In order to objectively analyze her results, she fixed a card on every key, blackened the performers' fingertips with ink, and collected the fingerprints they left.

> It was in 1895 [writes Catherine Pozzi], on the left bank of the Seine, *rue de Tournon*, that I saw once again the large, slightly dim salon where the great shadows of the Senate never allowed the daylight to enter fully. The piano alone caught our eye. It was the sole *raison d'être*, the entire life of this house. Such a peculiar atmosphere surrounded it that it seemed different from any other piano in the world. Half-covered with sheets of paper flowing with a firm hand-writing, some of its keys were covered with paper slips (held by an elastic) on which fingerprints in printing ink marked the hieroglyphs of a new language, its black and white mass seemed to be animated by a dominating, attractive and enchanted power...

---

93. Jaëll, Marie. *Méthode du Toucher*, p.18

This study of fingerprints led Marie Jaëll to precise conclusions. Where there is a coordination of contacts, that is to say, continuous ordering of papillary lines, there is harmony of play; where the fingerprints are disordered, without continuity, the sonority was poor, fingers were positioned without any harmony of contact, they were stiff, taut. The piano only gives back what it receives. If one sends it a finger that is aggressive, un-consenting or unsure, the sound, sent back, will be of the same nature, dry,[94] strong or timid, without resonance. In contrast, if we touch the piano with fingers that are free, happy to abandon themselves on the keyboard, harmoniously arranged, the sound will be open, resounding, full, warm, and timbred. The differences of the extent of the contact between the finger and the touch, as well as the localization of this contact at the fingertip, noticeably modify the sonority.

The timbres vary by infinitely delicate gradations according to the position and pressure of fingers. It is up to the pianist to learn to exploit such diversity in order to enhance the richness, coloring and expressiveness of his playing.

Liszt intuitively adopted the most physiological positions of the hand. He was often surprised when people attributed to him a particularly large hand. In reality, his hands were exactly proportional to his physical stature. However, thanks to his intuitive use of his hands, his different way of placing them, he triumphed over pianistic challenges. And the touch method shows how to hold one's hands at the piano.

Marie Jaëll's examination of the fingerprints on the keys helped her show that the superiority of great artists was inherent in their capacity to experience marvelous aural sensations and no less marvelous sensations of touch. This touch can be compared to that of a painter wielding his favorite brush, the writer who cannot

---

94. Jaëll, Marie. *L'intelligence et rythme dans,* p.9

compose without his familiar pen or pencil in hand; it's the same for a pianist at his keyboard as a violinist with his bow.

An imperfection in the form of touch, that is, an undesirable geometry of the design of fingerprints, brings a lack of harmony. "The placement of contacts plays an important role in the dexterity of fingers, since by grouping the contacts differently, we make the fingers more skilful for the execution of the same intervals. If we add to this fact the benefit of obtaining a beautiful sonority, it seems that the placement of contacts is meant to become the essential basis of musical education."[95] And in order to be able to localize and to vary the coordination of keys, the fingers need to be independent.

The dissociation of fingers is therefore a first skill to be acquired. It is indispensable to render the five fingers of the hand, usually distracted and unconscious, individually conscious and dissociated. That is not as simple as it sounds.

If, on opening the hand, we try to bend a finger individually, we will see how clumsy we are, and incapable of achieving this simple flexion without reflex of the other fingers. Each finger is an individual who must learn to act without the involuntary associated movements of other fingers. In a pianist who learns finger movements through automatic and unconscious procedures, there is a waste of motive activity. If we filmed how he plays, in slow motion, we would see evidence of the disorder of his movements. It would show all his fingers moving at the same time: those that are playing and those that are not. The fingers that are making useless and superfluous movements are like people chattering during a speech, saying nothing but detracting from the main event.[96] A close observation of the fingers of certain players at the piano reveals a multiplicity of movements to play just one piece. Such silent attacks are a waste of motive activity.

For the pianist it is also takes concentrated thought to render the keys elastic and to make the movements of his arms light. "Just

---

95. Jaëll, Marie. *Mécanisme du Toucher*

96. Jaëll, Marie, collectif Symétrie, édition de musique et services aux musiciens.

as a bird, at the moment it perches on a branch, softens the movement of its wings in order to avoid a shock, a pupil must also avoid the shock between his finger and the key." The finger's strike of the key must be rapid at the maximum, but its withdrawal must be slightly slower, like an elastic ball that rebounds from the ground. Elasticity, non-heaviness are the conditions essential for the harmonics of play.

If a pianist lets his finger, hand or arm with all its weight, the force serves only to hit the key; it is lost for the following movement, and there is no rebound. Such a process is contrary to the principle of elasticity that we naturally carry within ourselves. If we feel an attraction upward simultaneously with the movement of the finger's depressing the key, the movement that is executed will become elastic, winged.

When the arm is lowered, it must have the sensation of an opposite force, neutralizing a part of its impact. Then the sound produced becomes vibrant and has good timbre. The weight that is not counterbalanced stifles the sound, and does not allow the harmonics to free themselves. This suspension helps the pianist exploit and distribute his energy harmoniously, and give free rein to his play.

If the movement of the fingertip begins *above* the key, it will be moving when it hits the key and jar the hammer into vibrating; the fingertip must be in contact with the key *before* it touches the key. The key is depressed by pulling the fingertip down and towards oneself.

Different types of touch influence key movement. One can depress the keys with the fingers initially resting on the key surface or hit the keys from a certain distance above. In a *legato* touch, with the finger initially resting on the key, the motion follows a smooth path with continuously increasing key velocity. In a *staccato* touch in *forte*, the finger strikes from a distance above the key and releases it immediately after the blow.

Since one must always be prepared to use any or all fingers simultaneously, they must be all at the key surface at the same time.

For all fingers to be in proper position at the same time, the hands must be turned inward with both the palm and back horizontal.

A pianist should avoid depressing the keys by moving the whole hand downwards. Such a hand motion involves larger, slower-moving muscles, and hence provides less sensitive control. It also compromises the independence of the fingers when balancing chords by imposing the same downward motion on all of them.

All hand movements (except sideways) to bring the fingers into a new position are suspect. Otherwise, when the thumb goes down the little finger tends to fly up, well above the key, and conversely. The advice, "keep your fingers close to the keys" must be made more precise: "keep your fingers *on* the keys." This means that in moving the hand sideways to a new position, two distinct movements are required. First, the hand and fingers are moved into position and in contact with the correct keys, and only then are the keys depressed. Any attempt to combine the two motions into one will bring the whole weight of the hand and arm crashing onto the keys (and quite possibly the wrong ones!) Slowly practicing the fastest possible movement to a new position has the advantage of embedding the correct movement in so-called "muscle memory," that is, the right "brain image" with a consequent improvement in both accuracy and memory.

The subtle control of dynamics is essential for the constant shading of melodic lines and for the balancing of chords. This is best achieved with the fingers alone. If the fingers are forced to work regularly, they acquire the necessary muscular strength surprisingly quickly, and contrary to intuition fingers alone can produce a bigger sound than any amount of arm action.

With a level wrist, the movement of the fingertip can easily be varied over the full range, from vertical to near horizontal. But high wrists do not allow for vertical motion. Before any note is played, the finger is in position with the tip in contact with the key surface. Only then is the key is depressed, solely by a pulling movement of the finger. Dynamics are controlled primarily by the angle at which the fingertip pushes the key down.

No one hand is similar to another, and it is difficult to imagine an ideal hand. Every and any hand can be considered to be harmonious. One must simply learn to transmit the manual harmony to the keyboard. "The most appropriate structure for the harmony of touch should be such as to make the harmony transmissible," concludes Marie Jaëll. To make the hand sensitive to transmission basically boils down to training it.

Marie Jaëll and Charles Féré were convinced that every finger possesses a sensation that is specific to it. In their view, training the hand meant learning how to isolate the sensations of each finger, sensations of movement and immobility; being able to feel the relations of sensations of fingers among themselves, and the relations of intervals. To that end, they developed a program of exercises called "away from the keyboard." Its objective is to help a pianist gradually obtain a complete dissociation of fingers.

Individualization is necessary if a pianist is to feel the useful influence that the activity of one finger can exercise on another finger. To awaken the hand is also to learn in large part to dissociate movement from immobility. The mastery of one's movements that helps fingers obtain the best touch, the most precise contact, is inseparably linked to improvements in immobility.

"Every organ that moves needs the support of an organ that does not move." The organs that are not involved in the action must also be trained to remain still. "On seeing persons who surround me, I am struck how many movements they make that are useless and not consciously linked to their thoughts and their actions."[97]

Thus Marie Jaëll recommended regular exercises *without* the piano, what she called "exercises in immobility." One such exercise consists in describing a circle with one finger, while keeping the others immobile; then, moving two fingers together but in the opposite direction, while keeping the others still. At first, the pupil may not succeed in moving the two fingers simultaneously, but only

---

97. Jaëll, Marie. *Méthode du Toucher*

in turns. One of the greatest difficulties is to communicate equal rhythm to the two movements.

"The keyboard is not made to render fingers independent, but to transmit independent movements of the fingers."[98] Thus the pianist has to learn to control two aspects of the same energy, motionlessness and movement of sound.

There is a parallel, here, to the *zen* painter, whose being lives off the sense and life of the flower he wishes to paint, before launching his brush on the canvas. "If you want to paint a flower, become a flower," he tells one of his pupils. Similarly, Marie Jaëll seems to tell her pupils, "before playing the sound, *be* the sound." The pianist's total attention builds up a tension within him and, conversely, his ability to recover such tension, and to be tuned in, reinforces his attention and listening. As he recovers perfect tension, and the state of inner resonance, he rediscovers the freedom of being one with his instrument.

In 1899, Jaëll published a new and more complete version of the method of touch, *Piano Teaching Based on Physiology*, in three volumes. Here, she worked to translate the discoveries she had made in association with Charles Féré on the physiology of the pianist, his fingerprints and their intimate link with the sense of touch into concrete measures for piano teaching. She introduced her method with these words:

> We have established the important role these minuscule sensory organs play in touch ... by means of a comparative analysis of a large number of fingerprints made by performers of all kinds. This accumulation of fingerprints has permitted the precise verification of the correlative position of the five fingers. It has allowed us to establish that:
> - the smallness (pettiness) of the contact with the keys which is found among most performers is one of the causes of the inferiority of touch.
> - flaws in sonority, rhythm and style correspond to a lack of correlation of digital lines of different fingerprints.

98.Ibidem

160

- in the case of harmonious playing, the fingerprints are in correlation with the perfect equilibrium of the hand's position.

By way of a conclusion, she writes, "If a great artist reaches the truth of the concordance of aural sensations and tactile sensations, such a concordance must necessarily become the basis of teaching."[99]

The three volumes contain the key principles of her method, and outline her main ideas on musical aesthetics. They lay the foundations for the initiation of a different kind of music, where all the faculties of the musician are called into play: aural, tactile, visual and mental. They explain how a musician can develop his sensitivity and capacity to allow himself to be touched by music.

In her follow-up books, Marie Jaëll would speak of her exploration of the still subtler means to fully develop the hand's sensitivity, and that of the human being as a whole. Little by little, her incursion into the world of multiple sensations that nurture man and link him to his intelligence took her to a universe where few of her friends could follow.

MY FINGERS TOUCH WHAT MY EYES SEE

Marie Jaëll now entered upon the most creative period of her life. Her approach to the touch focused at first on absolute pitches and harmony. She had explained how her technique could reveal the pitch and timbre of a single note at a particular dynamic level. Now she undertook a study of rhythm and melody, the horizontal dimension of music. Now music's thematic, textural and expressive issues took center-stage in her pedagogy.

Coming after her remarkable results on finger movements and their related brain-images involved in piano playing, it came as a delight and a surprise when she learned that vision also played a critical role in her touch technique. She found that the source of the

99.Ibidem

161

rhythmic transformations actuating the pianist's fingers lies in the rhythmic movements of his eyes as they read the music text. This discovery led her to her next topic of research.

She was venturing into new waters, but always buoyed by her lofty belief that music is intentional movement. Her enquiry on the sense of touch persuaded her of the importance of that view for piano playing. Now, she focused on the deep links that join the visual and tactile sensations in piano music. She argued that the pianist's eyes as they read the notes must capture the rhythm and melody they express. These are then instantly passed on to the fingers by the brain. The finger and eye movements are partners that work together to project the ideas and emotions embedded in the music. They sustain each other through mutual feedback.

Most musical analysis, fixated on harmony, deals almost exclusively with pitch, and rhythm is left by the wayside.[100] Most analysis pays greatest attention to the pitches themselves, independent of any instrumental color. Some performers make matters worse as they shrug away the composers' directions for tempo, pedal use and fingering as mere "suggestions" that may be brushed aside. Once more, the danger exists that piano playing can becoming a mechanical exercise lacking in thought and inspiration.

Luckily, true pianists are not technicians but artists. They are not content to play individual notes in a flashy, virtuoso style. They sense that a pitch is a stretch of sound with a clear and stable frequency that is related to the overall rhythm of the piece. And all musical work is a coherent pattern of pitches bound together with the melody as the leitmotif. Indeed, every pitch has a duration, and every duration is part of a rhythm. Just a single piano note can be a pointer to the structure of the entire piece.

Consequently Marie Jaëll's study of harmony was not confined to describing and cataloguing the local phenomena of music. She enlarged her enquiry in order to highlight the themes that form the lifeblood of music. She started with rhythm and melody. She

---

100. Rosen, C. "The Future of Western Music," *The New York Review of Books*

brought the two together in her concept of music as directed movement where rhythms create movement and melody gives direction. Since voice, as the driving force of musical gestures, is absent in piano music, she explored how body movements can invest music with style and indicate its intentionality. In this way her touch method can point to the intricate relationships binding the different notes in a chord, such as their overlaps and their relative strengths, fix their timing in, and underscore, the melody line. In her view the mastery of such factors underlay the success shown by leading pianists like Liszt.

She took one of the peculiar properties of rhythm as the starting point for her study of rhythms in piano music. She noted that piano music "unwinds time," by simulating it. It is heard sound by sound and the idea that animates it unravels in time. The tempo of its sounds, constituting the "events" of musical experience, consists of formal devices such as cyclicity, repetition, and contrast variation. In this way perceptual impressions of extension or compression are created.

She contrasted time-driven music to paintings and sculptures that are space-bound. When we admire a painting, we first see it as a whole, and then we take in its details at leisure. But when we start listening to a piece of music, we have no inkling how it will unfold. What struck Marie Jaëll, as she listened to Liszt playing, was the invisible presence of a perspective to the sounds emanating from his music. A solitary musical phrase in his playing seemed to give a picture of the whole piece. She felt as if her mind had taken wings and flown forward and backward, along pathways unknown to her, and painted a picture of the music being played. She thought that such a phenomenon could be created whenever someone plays the piano; one has only to see the spatial dimension built into it. The accomplished pianist's eyes "see" the music, which thus becomes a visual art. Here, seeing is understanding, and understanding is creating.

Her investigations into piano aesthetics delved deep into rhythm as an essential component of all music. Indeed, the music of every epoch and every culture consists of more or less rhythmically ordered tones. These rise and fall metaphorically or stay the same, and then combine simultaneously or in sequence. She saw rhythmic movement driven by harmony as the essence of piano music.

Nature was her starting point. Here she followed in the footsteps of the great Romantic composers like Liszt, Chopin and Schumann who took inspiration from Nature for their musical work. The manifold rhythms that pervade the life of all beings fascinated her. She spent long hours observing trees and admiring their movements as a wind fluttered their leaves, as if it were breathing life into them.

She remarked that rhythms are an intrinsic trait of nature, whether we mean plants, animals or humans. Rhythms are present everywhere in recurring phenomena like the seasons, days and nights, ocean tides, bird-songs, the utterances of a frog, breath and heartbeats. According to her, rhythmic oscillations are the core of all reality, and the rhythmic sounds that suffuse nature reveal a profound bond among all living beings.

She noted that there is more to rhythms than mere repetition. All of them represent similar phenomena, yet are not absolutely identical. When nature picks up a geometric form, for example flower petals or snow crystals, it seems to be carried away by a certain wild fancy and revels in profligacy. The symmetry of recurring shapes in the tides of the sea and the delicate tracery of veins upon a leaf reflect unity in diversity. Their infinite variations constitute creative as well as aesthetic elements. It is precisely in these irregularities of nature that life, and the beauty of its forms, speak loudest. They exchange symmetries and inject new dynamism into nature.

The analogy between piano music and the tides can be pushed further.[101] A large wave and many smaller waves are borne by the same tide — but the two move in opposite directions. In piano music, movements through closely related tonalities represent small

---

101.Hopkins, A. *Understanding Music*, p.44.

waves and back-and-forth motions. They are all carried forward by the principal modulation that gives them direction. One can visualize such a pattern of rhythms as a packing of smaller and smaller circles within a large circle but moving in different directions.

As a result the rhythmic periods overlap and blend. They are like the myriad leaves of a tree that resemble but can never replicate each other exactly. Every phenomenon in life is thus unique. Rhythm, which is a succession of unique phenomena is, in its totality, a unique and personal movement. And because it is life, it eschews routine.

"In Nature," she jotted in her notebook, "no movement remains uniform. The waterfalls, the forests enlivened by the swinging of trees, the undulating sea waves are all marvelous combinations of rhythms. We stare at such wonderful phenomena, enthralled, but we do not try to analyze the multiplicity of their rhythms. The rhythmic phenomena in Nature attract the least of our attention."[102]

But her attention was piqued. Stimulated by her observations, she prepared a new book that appeared in 1904: *Intelligence and Rhythm in Artistic Movements*. This volume, too, was a popular success.

Her reflections spurred her on to raise questions about the rhythmic currents that permeate and give life to works of art, be they musical, pictorial or architectural. She stressed that rhythm in a work of art is what gives life to space, structure and image. It is the creative spark that lights up all works of art, and music in particular.

Her new work was far more complex than her earlier books. It starts with rhythm, a phenomenon that intrigued and enticed her. Seeking to elucidate its central role in music, she goes on to uncover the multiple links and mutual impacts among the different tactile, aural and visual sensations unleashed by music. Her one goal is to discover the laws common to all of them.

---

102. Jaëll, Marie. *L'intelligence et le rythme dans les mouvements artistiques*

The book describes in the minutest detail her musings on the intrinsic links between artistic movement and musical thought. She argues that one's consciousness of a movement triggers thought, and awakens intelligence. But it is important to note that a movement's value lies largely in the thought animating it; it is thought that endows it with expressive force and life.

> Movement in itself is a support to thought, on condition that it should not be uniform, but what is a uniform movement if not a movement that has no goal to attain, therefore no origin, no life, no finish, no breath?[103]

To her, the more thought there is underlying the music, the more tightly the notes are held together by hidden forces. These results underwrite her aesthetics of piano music.

One of her friends, a piano professor in Colmar, wrote a letter to her that takes us deep into the subtlety of Marie's research.

> Dear Marie, on reading your book I often had the impression, which Pasteur's disciples must have had when he introduced them to the universe of the infinitely small, a universe invisible to the naked eye, where, however, all is organization, all is life. It is impossible for me to feel with my hand the infinite subtleties you speak of, just as it is impossible for me to see with my eyes the bacilli, the microbes. I have no microscope. My tactile sensations, in contrast to yours, are crude, just as my sight is limited when left to its own resources. The unceasing and intense work to which you devote yourself has produced in you a microscope which lets you observe and analyze the infinitesimal fractions about which ordinary mortals have not the least idea, the faintest hint. Everything that has been done in this field is nothing compared to your method of work. Future generations will reap, I hope, the fruit of the seeds of your labor...[104]

---

103. *Ibidem*
104. Kiener

Most of all, Marie Jaëll pointed out the secret affinity between nature's rhythms and man's brain activity. From the window of her room, she would watch the treetops sway to and fro. They seemed to be stirred by distinct forces. In her imagination she could also sense how their trunks of different girths put up varying degrees of resistance to the wind whose intensity varied and shifted as it brushed each treetop. Then it dawned on her that the harmony reigning among them had its counterpart in her thinking. The observation of all rhythmic phenomena made her feel, see and consequently think. She became convinced that rhythms create a reciprocity between the outer world and man's inner being.

She took her analysis further. There are two distinct processes at work when a person's gaze perceives rhythms. During the first stage the brain decomposes and analyzes the rhythmic differences. During the second stage it restores them in the unity of time. Such a capacity may be fundamental in the development of human intelligence. Indeed, the rhythmic unity of a movement, of a musical measure, in fact of all artistic phenomena, are fully grasped only when the mind knows how to discern its most minute variations in time. Behind the possibility of rhythmic divisions, down to infinitesimal level, highlighted by an analysis of eye movements, lies the unifying force that activates our thought under the influence of all sensory perceptions and externalizes them. Eye movements reflect the smallest gradation and modification of rhythms.

Once more, Marie Jaëll's program appeals to consciousness since the perception of time is born out of the relation of the self to the universe. She harks back to the idea that consciousness is constituted in time and unfolds in time. In the development of the consciousness of time, there are two main experiences, each with distinct traits: succession and duration. Both are infinitesimal and occur in split milliseconds. They mobilize "micro-consciousnesses" that are almost unconscious, and then mysteriously form the consciousness.

When the Greeks recognized rhythm in music, what held their attention was not the rhythm of flux or flow but the pause, the reiterated limitation of movement. They argued that rhythm imposes constraints on movement and the flux of things, and thus constructs the pattern of movement. According to them, rhythm, a periodic occurrence, is the primordial ground of time. The brain also has an inbuilt inhibition in the form of selective neurons that mark out a path for vision to perceive.

In line with such a view, Marie Jaëll concluded that rhythm is the temporal organization of music as its pace quickens. It can be defined as a sequence of movements that harmonize and recur without ever repeating exactly. The essence of rhythm is a return, in some sense. It is movement, renewal, and similarity whose recurrence does not lapse into absolute regularity.

"Measure," Liszt was wont to say, "is to music what rhythm is to poetry; it is not the forced cadence that weighs on the caesura. One should not imprint a uniform movement on music but impart life to it by consciously speeding and slackening, following the sense it conveys." It was while listening to him play that Marie Jaëll realized for the first time the subtlety of such rhythmic differentiation.

"I must say, it was not the music as composed by its creator that I was listening to but to its ideal transfiguration, a music infinitely more beautiful, infinitely more divisible whose minute gradations of rhythms and nuances could no longer be translated by the written notation."[105] Thus Marie Jaëll introduces the topic of the transcription of rhythms on a sheet of paper.

Her new topic tackled the critical confrontation between word and sound that has bedevilled Western music since the Renaissance. To start with, there is an important distinction between "tone" as sound and "note" as the written element symbolizing it. The inventories of notes, indicating roughly the different sounds that a musical instrument is designed to emit, form the building blocks of a musical idiom. The rhythm of a musical piece is quantitatively organized by means of the material measure

105. Jaëll, Marie. *L'intelligence et le rythme*

of long and short beats in terms of duration. The time units used are half notes, quarter notes and dotted quarter notes, and the beats, spaced equally in time. The rate at which these last occur defines the tempo, a quantity that varies over time and is specific to each musical work.

Musical composers are masters of a highly specialized language. The syntax of harmony, based on vertical sonority, is organized around triads of two thirds and fifths. It gives prominence to the third, and to its complementary fifth, in order to form new configurations. Such a structure expresses rest, and at the same time cries out for movement. It combines and it moves forward. In this way it regulates the flow of sounds into a systematic rhythmic pattern. It also offers the possibility of subdividing the musical language through the repetition of rhythmic patterns and thus creating the illusion of continuity. At this micro-level, it is broken apart into syllables. The pianist's task is to put them all together in a new way and re-construct a whole in order to recreate the musical piece.

In any context, the musical sentence as a unit is a meaningful combination of syntactic elements. But its transcription on paper does not indicate how it should be rendered. The notes constituting it are represented on the paper by distinct points. They have no life in common. What is noted down is the result of composition in the narrowest sense. Consequently, music in writing cannot suggest the subtleties and the minute variations of the rhythmic current that runs through a piece of music. Even the precise quality of the intervals is not revealed there. The notation is a map, of sorts, for the performer. Beethoven and Chopin indicated the structure of the phrase by marking the finger and pedal movements, and metronome marks were often essential to their conceptions. Unfortunately, other composers failed to follow their example.

A gulf therefore lies between notation and music as sound. Deciphering the notation is not the same as recreating the music. The meaning of a musical work is contained not in the silent notation alone but in the invisible threads and shapes crying out to the pianist. The notes, thought out by the musician, influence each other in terms of duration and intensity. They come together and they move apart by infinitesimal gradation. The notes do not reveal the linking fluid influences; but the musician perceives them and helps others to perceive them.

Marie Jaëll concluded that the values of the notes as given by musical notation are in reality only a conventional approximation. She compared a musical phrase to a molecule whose constituent atoms are bonded together by forces of attraction. Sounds do not just succeed each other; between them there is an attraction. The phenomenon of rhythmic grouping is not physical but mental. Therefore a pianist, as he reads the music text, must intuit its underlying rhythmic subtleties. This perspective explains why Marie Jaëll held a lax attitude with respect to the actual pitch content of music. She appealed to pianists' imagination to overcome "the basic antagonism of score to performance, of concept to realization that is the glory of Western music."[106]

"We have 'uniform' measures...It is up to the musician interpreter to break through the barrier of uniformity, and rediscover the true rhythmic values of a piece."[107] "If the notes are progressively close or far removed from each other, accordingly, as the underlying rhythm speeds up or slows down, the eye can read them musically. The minute differences of the duration would be identified with the minute differences of dimensions."

To the uninitiated, musical notes are esoteric and are nothing but discrete points. But they stand for the visual dimension of music. They instantly initiate a visual dialogue with the pianist. The rhythmic elements they describe catch his attention and he sees there lines, spirals, loops and circles. In this way Marie came to notice the analogy between the rhythms of music and of eye movements.

---

106. Rosen, C. "The Future of Music," *The New York Review of Books*, Dec. 20, 2001

107. Jaëll, M., *Musique et Psychophysiologie*

Her viewpoint led her to conclude that the sight-reading of music is a mental activity. She was astonished to find the mental processes that command the finger pressures on the keys also order the eye movements. She probed the human mind and its visual pathways with the techniques of piano music. She discovered new inter-locking relations among aural, visual and tactile sensations.

She remarked that even the most elementary act of looking at a tree or a straight line on a piece of paper is an active process. Once again, consciousness steps in since we perceive an object only if we are conscious of it and do not perceive it if we are not conscious of it. Just like the hands, the eyes build brain-images of nature. During the formation of visual images, the brain is not a passive chronicler of the external physical reality but actively constructs it. To see is to understand and go to the heart of things.

Man's visual system has evolved over millions of years. The images it builds are stored and reinterpreted as new data come in. Children learn by themselves and reinvent the visual world in three dimensions before they walk. One imagines vision to be seamless, giving the illusion of continuity of a flowing mobile consciousness. In reality, it is a fusing of discrete perceptions. When stripped deep down it consists of micro-conscious events. In the fraction of a second we detect a great deal and capture the multiple facets of reality. Our gaze can change directions in 20 to 150 milliseconds with an angular speed of 800° per second. And Marie Jaëll zoomed in for a detailed microscopic analysis of the visual world.

When we look at an object, the eyes perceive its color, then its form and lastly its movement. These three traits are distinct and have specific areas in the brain for their processing. Given her view of music as rhythmic movement, Marie Jaëll's prime interest was directed to movements in her analysis of sight-reading. Then she associated forms and colors to them.

When we see an object, we always see it against the backdrop of what surrounds it, just as we hear a tone along with all its overtones. The brain has a built-in ability to compare various elements in the field of view, process them and then put together.

Marie Jaëll began by considering how the eyes behave when perceiving lines, rectangles, squares, circles and spirals. She observed the variations in eye movements as they look at the same object and move upwards or downwards, from right to left or from left to right. The visual brain has highly selective neurons to capture the different rhythms for a line of specific orientation, or motion in a specific direction. Several distinct rhythms in time can correspond to one and the same form in space. The forms may be parallel or perpendicular lines, diagonal lines, curves resolving into straight lines or spirals; the speed of the gaze remains variable during the total trajectory. It picks up acceleration and loses it as the orientation changes from right to left or left to right. Specific cells in the cortex are specialized to capture both the direction and orientation of objects

The brain is amazing in its capacity to integrate information. It brings together the results of the different visual processing systems and gives a unitary image of the visual world. Marie Jaëll argued that the rhythmic diversity, revealed by an analysis of eye movements, seems to represent the unified force that activates our thought through sensory perceptions and manifests itself through them. There is a correlation between the appreciation of forms and the rhythmic character of eye movements. In addition, a modification in the orientation of lines provokes corresponding rhythmic modification in the pace of the gaze. The eye movements adapt themselves precisely to changes in linear contours.

The perception of orientation that depends on eye movements is a remarkable fact. Its close link with the orientation of tactile sensations is more significant for the touch method. It was a revelation to find that movements of the fingers and hands can also provoke changes in the orientation of eye movements. Marie Jaëll arrived at this realization by watching the gestures of two masons from the vantage point of her apartment. Dressed in white, they spent a whole year repairing a white stone staircase. Their least movements cast sharp shadows on their white uniforms. She distinguished not only the start and the end of successive movements. She used the circle formed by her thumb and index fingers as a kind of lens to focus their impulses and decompose them into minute fractions. To her astonishment a secret harmony transfigured their action. Their apparently monotonous, simple gestures recalled a swinging pendulum with continuously varying speeds, representing rhythmic diversity joined to a fundamental unity. They were elements of a work of art. She then noted that a deep similarity existed between the manual actions of an artisan and an artist. Our hands and our eyes build the images of nature and endow them with artistic beauty by charging them with emotions.

The brain constructs images from rhythmic appearances. These may be fleeting, but they leave behind impressions that will not be effaced. Thus the memory builds up its store of forms indefinitely. The gaze follows the orientation of the images, and the images are nothing but orientations. The eyes see the forms not merely in the space they occupy but also in their evolution in time. Here, time means movement, the actual well as the illusory, that is perceived through the indication of lines and shapes in the objects.

Finally, Marie Jaëll put colors on the forms. She noticed that to put movement as a perceptual phenomenon into color relationships is to put order into ideas. This notion came to her on studying the enlarged hand of La Victoire de Rudé. From there it was just one step to the realization that the experience of color is closely interwoven with the experience of music. She began to use colors to capture the sensitivity of fingertips.

She presented her conclusions in her next book, called *A new State of Consciousness, the Coloring of Tactile Sensations*. She argued that fingers become more sensitive when given an appropriate color. The colors become a language to give expression and meaning to our perceptions. Thanks to them one feels the keys as never before and hear the sounds and their timbres as never before. She became convinced that colors do have an influence on the education of the hand. She tested her ideas by looking at a luminous circle; she found her eye movements speeding up while they moved up along the circumference and slackening while they moved down.

Finally, she returned to eye movements in relation to musical texts. With all their notation, musical texts contain all the rhythms in the form of circles, lines and spirals. The notes contain the sensory and motor aspects of musical memory. Neuroscience finds that musical sight-reading and keyboard performance activate the cortical areas that are adjacent to, though not identical with, Wernerniche's area and Broca's area, respectively.[108] Finger movements and musical notes form the elements of a single integrated process. In piano music, the fingers play what the eyes see.

Thus Marie Jaëll turned to the topic of developing the musicality of vision. She also observed that her fingers adapted their movements quite docilely to the successive rhythmic transformations suffered by the visual sensation. She had a feeling that the eyes transmitted their rhythms to the keys. Guided by the rhythmic images of the visual evolution, she heard the unfolding of a musical rhythm in the purest form.

There is indeed a deep link between the rhythms of music suggested by the text and the rhythms of the gaze. So there is a need to educate the eyes, and perfect their movements, as well as the hands.

Marie Jaëll talked about perfecting the musicality of the gaze, about learning to analyze the rhythmic transformations that manifest in eye movements and in general in the movements we perceive. She proposed a series of visual exercises designed to perfect eye movements in relation to finger movements. In her view the pianist experiences directed rhythmic movements most intensely when his visual and tactile impressions work together and confirm each other.

She noted that in spite of any effort we might make, we cannot uninterruptedly think through or conceptualize a movement, even when we want to make it completely uniform. The breaks that are typical of mental functions indicate that the thought process is

---

108. Fuster, J.M., *Menos in the Cerebral Cortex*, MIT Press. 1999 p 141

blocked by the mechanization that we want to communicate to the movement. In contrast, when a movement seems to be heading towards a goal, with a slightly accelerated pace, thought identifies itself with it and flows freely. "Movement and thought complement each other...Little by little thought seems to become the body whose movement is nothing but its shadow."[109]

Marie Jaëll gives the example of a circular line along which our vision circulates freely. "If you allow your vision to follow the circular line, without directing its pace, it established differentiated speeds, that is to say, every time it goes around the eyes gradually slow their pace while going up and then accelerate, also gradually, on the way down, so that you see not only the form in the space that it occupies but you feel it, you count it in time. There is a fusion between the representation of the rhythm in time and the representation of the form in space."[110] Thus the motion should not be uniform; otherwise, there would be no divisions of space in time any more, nor would there be any rhythm.

That means that the pianist, as he reads the music text written down by the composer, must visualize it as an ideal transfiguration of the underlying music and render it infinitely more beautiful by going in for infinitely more refinement. The infinite divisions of the rhythms and nuances, those that cannot be translated by the signs of music in writing, produce the most profound and lasting impressions.

In her book Marie Jaëll goes much farther. She even suggests the possibility of a revolution in music notation — for the cluster of notes and their shape cannot tell us much. The relation of notation to realization is selective. The appearance of the notes has a specific suggestive effect upon the player. It is their grouping that identifies a regular rhythmic pattern. An innovation in music writing could indicate visual sensations to assist our sense of sight in feeding information to the mind, and the hand. She proposed that musical

---

109. Jaëll, Marie. *Intelligence et Rythmes* p.18
110. Jaëll, Marie. *Intelligence et Rythmes* p.25

notation should be such that the performer could safely trust his eyes to instantly sense the music's rhythm. Such a change could help the pianist capture a more comprehensive and lively understanding of the rhythm.

Hence, it is not surprising that Marie Jaëll asked her pupils to memorize the written musical text, consciously. Then, they could remember only the rhythms and thoughts constituting the music, and as they were playing, when movements occur in milliseconds, they would not read the music; they could let the dynamics of the music lead them on. Spontaneously and naturally, the pianist becomes the music.

Musical notes are played and heard as discrete events, with a beginning and an end, with an objective of height or color of the sound. Such a property sets music apart from sequences of sound that are part of a continuous pattern, high or low, like the blowing of the wind, an engine roar or the intonations of speech. In man-made music, the whole is more than the sum of the parts; there is an overarching idea running through it. Underlying the succession of notes there is a deeper and more essential character. An artist singles that out and brings it to life.

Marie Jaëll's analysis led her to focus on what is called "expressive music performance." Even today, "it is a poorly understood phenomenon in spite of its importance both from a musical and a cognitive perspective."[111] To obtain it, a pianist has to creatively read the written score of a musical piece and modify gradually or abruptly the tempo or loudness at certain places to communicate its musical message and emotion. To weave a piece of music into a cohesive and continuous picture, he must learn the musical reading of the text and capture its intelligibility and expression.

---

111. Dixon, S. et al., "The Performance Worm", *Journal of Acoustical Society of America*, July 2001

THE PARADISE OF THE GOD *Indra*

Piano music mirrors the universe of beings linked to each other by invisible rhythmic bonds. It re-actualizes the deep communion between man and nature. To help a pianist enter that paradise, Marie Jaëll's touch method envisions the fusion among the representations of rhythms in time and of forms in space. Such a process mobilizes his entire being, and unlike other musicians, a pianist feels intensely the sounds his performance produces.

Music is harmony and rhythm, and above all the melody that is the message. As they play a chord of harmony, pianists are confronted with a subtle problem of indicating the melody. As a finale, Marie Jaëll explains how her touch method is best suited to highlight the intentionality and thought underlying music. But the essence of performing music is in the making of music, and all musical interpretation culminates in the actual realization of sound.

Most music establishes a key, a base note or tonic that establishes a home from which the melody takes off and to which it returns. Melody is always interpreted at the source and destination. It sends messages that are encoded in music and are decodable by the human heart. Above all, it speaks the language of feeling, and so elicits feeling.

Melody in the tonal system clearly implies a simultaneous combination of sounds, such as major and minor triads. Hence, it is fundamentally inseparable from harmony, since it strings together different pitches into a coherent whole. The melody lead is the opening motif, which is not only heard again later but is re-interpreted when it appears again in the movement. It is essential for the pianist to be able to shape a piece of music and indicate its musical structure and emotion, and through nuances of touch he can shape it very subtly.

Melody emphasis can arise in three ways, since a chord is composed of sequences of pitches organized in three different ways, all at the same time. Each pattern of organization is captured in a mental representation: the first is a grouping structure; the second is a metrical structure with the repeating sequence of strong and weak beats; the third structure dissects the melody into essential parts and ornaments. Thus the melody can be singled out by prolongation, reiteration or recurrence of certain pitches to which others are fundamentally subordinate. Jaëll suggested a device that could be called the melody lead.[112] It depends on differences of the pitches, which a pianist can control. Since he *lives* the music he is going to play, he goes beyond what is prescribed in the written score and modifies the tempo or loudness, gradually or abruptly. That is his way of guiding a listener to identify a musical piece in a multi-voiced environment.

Her method is also akin to what the pianists now call "velocity artifact." It consists in stressing one voice in a chord as the pianist's fingers push the keys down but giving different accelerations. Her instincts told her that there is a deep link between two contacts: the finger pushing the key to the key-bed and the hammer impacting on the string. Modern experiments show that there are consistently high correlations between the timing of the finger-key contact and the strong overall dependency of melody lead on acceleration. Thus the hammers arrive at the strings at different times. The strings that give the melody notes are struck earlier than others by around 30 milliseconds. If the dynamic differences are larger, the extent of melody lead is greater. In Marie Jaëll's touch method, this technical expertise must be consciously acquired and internalized.

After explaining how a pianist should play by paying attention to harmony and rhythm, Marie Jaëll describes what a piano teacher should do and not do. No longer is he to force his pupils to concentrate systematically on mechanical fingerings. His job is not to hand out ready-made tricks that a pupil might be tempted to assimilate by a routine of repetition and mechanics. There is a danger that rigorous instrumental training can squelch innate musical creativity. Even musically gifted children become miserable and obstinate when faced with endless repetition. They lose heart

---

112. Goebble

when they are asked to string notes together correctly, over and over, and reproduce music written by someone else. Above all the teacher should avoid interpreting the musical piece for his pupils.

The teaching of piano is then transformed into a mission of awakening. Children, whose brains are musically wired, are creative and commonly make up tunes at the piano by the age of five. Consequently the pedagogue's work takes on a new dimension. He guides the beginner to activate his intelligence (which is defined as taking an active attitude in reacting to new situations — to innovate, to invent the means and to adapt oneself without end), and helps him grasp the different elements that compose it. The ideal in piano teaching is to encourage the pupil, whether adult or child, to find within himself the responses, the attitudes that will help him overcome the difficulties, be they of technical order, of musical understanding or of touch.

Thus, little by little the pupil himself discovers the right responses. He is in a position then to ask "his" questions later on. He learns to think with his hand. He becomes a full being, capable of exploiting his potential, and creating for himself a fund of personal knowledge. Children instinctively sense the relationship that prevails between succession and duration that is at the core of music.

> A child has such a wealth of germs within him that he is often misunderstood. We seek to communicate our personal knowledge to him instead of showing him how, by his own resources, he can build up a capital of personal knowledge. It is by teaching the child to know himself that one ought to make known to him all that is outside him.[113]

At last Jaëll presents her vision of piano playing. She brings together all the components of music and adds to them immobility and silence. Then she makes a synthesis of them.

---

113. Jaëll, Marie. *L'intelligence et le rythme*

Finally, Marie Jaëll suggests how the touch method should disclose the rhythm underlying the music. To her, music is a movement with orientation given by the melody. Movement involves both space and time, since it has a beginning and an end. We normally perceive the direction of time through harmonic changes. The course of the entire movement can be broken up into several elements: acceleration, deceleration, each with its own *raison d'être*. This living decomposition of the movement entails a natural respiration that is rhythm, which Marie Jaëll called rhythmic current.

First, she looks at space and time in order to give a spatial perspective to music. In her conception of music, space is central. Expressiveness in music is double, owing to movement, movement in virtual space, and movement in time proper; the space is illusory and elusive but essential; in it, music takes shape moving through time. In a sense, pianists eradicate time with their rhythmic tricks. They immerse themselves in sound that defies time and structure by going deep within it.

Space perception is connected with vision, while temporal ordering is linked to hearing. In piano music the time factor steps in as soon as we subdivide its movements across space. There will be a beginning, a middle that is a carryover, and an end, which itself is an overture to another beginning. Each phrase answers and gently melts into the following one. All musical meaning is conveyed by the intervals: the not-yet, the now and the afterward.

Exactly in the same way, immobility is also central to movement. Every time we try to intensify our perceptions, we become tense. We strain our ears to hear better, all our being becomes taut with the effort to feel, see, perceive better, and for that we stand still. It is a sinewy stillness, different from repose. There is strength in being still in the moment. The consciousness and mastery of immobility by suppressing useless movements end in perfect movement, and give the pianist a more intense listening. Such immobility is comparable to silence, an active silence at whose core is elaborated all profound thought.

Piano music contains silence at its core. It is a drama of discrete sounds enveloped in a continuum of deep silence. In the midst of silence, music sounds intense, clear and sensuous. The pure experience of sound in relation to silence is akin to the loss of experience of light in relation to darkness.

The pianist has precision instruments at his disposal to situate himself in time and space before his instrument: his tactile, aural and visual sensations of rhythmic movements. By being conscious of all the details that fire up his sensations in the three dimensional space he can grasp most profoundly the rhythm of the piece he is interpreting.

A pianistic movement, a gesture, for example the strike of a touch, a curve over the keyboard, a glide along it, all unleash a universe of sensations:

Sensation of the pads of the fingertips
Contact with the ivory keys
Sensation of space
Relation of distances

This sensory awareness pervades us, and reaching the brain triggers it to new awareness. "Where there is sensation, there is a gleam of thought." Sensation-thought unity exists; one has only to discover it.

Thus, the pianist's gaze sees the rhythms and reads the musical language in its abstracted written form, and the fingers are activated. What carries the pianist forward is the rhythm. The brain activity deployed by the musician is capable of evoking on the keyboard the musical harmony perceived, first, visually.

How do space and time intervene in the execution of movements and in the thinking of the musician? The first space a pianist learns to know is the one between his body and the keyboard. Then comes the space of the keyboard itself, which he should perceive not only laterally (breadth) but also in depth (striking the keys), and in height (withdrawing the fingers from the keys, bending over the keyboard). When he is comfortable in this realm, he lets his hands and arms move around in a three dimensional space in which he registers the dance of his movements, the march of his thought.

In this way, piano music becomes dance. The graceful and dramatic movements of the arm and wrists of the performer describe a kind of choreography. His gestures serve a double function. First, there is the visual effect on the audience; his physical signs tell the audience what the performer is feeling and supplement the message conveyed by the actual sound. Even the most emphatic final cadence will sometimes fail to prepare the audience for the fact that the music is coming to an end, without some kind of visual indication. Without that, the applause all performers hope for will be late in coming — and perhaps less enthusiastic, as the drama of the moment is lost! Second, and more important, dramatic displays of physical prowess in piano music (as in ballet) have an artistic importance. They become an integral part of the interpretation. Louder sounds always entail larger and faster body movements like hands and arms softer tones require smaller more controlled movements

Music, like dance, takes its meaning from and gives meaning to time and space. Both mobilize the performer's entire being. Etymologically, rhythm means "flow," or flux, like the current of a river... The flow of a musical rhythm is a current whose movement is not restricted by a channel or canal; it can be rapid or slow; a musician sails on it, at the mercy of eddies and swirls, attentive to the life he perceives. Hovering over his keyboard, the pianist abandons himself, light and ethereal, to be borne along by the currents that pervade all musical work, free to be wafted to and fro along the multiple directions of harmonies. Thus, his physical display becomes part of the drama.

> To give expression, by a movement of the least dimension [says Marie Jaëll], "is to enhance the consciousness of it, and to intensify its expression. Truly, it is the most minute, the subtlest motive, tactile and aural sensations that demand the greatest mental exercise. The operations of the mind are invisible, elusive, infinitely

delicate; but we know how powerful their effects are. Man has locked up his greatest force in his thought.[114]

Such a view highlights the fact that there are no limits to perfecting the acquisition of the divisibility of space with respect to the form and duration of artistic movements. "For thought, by progressively refining sensations and movements, divides the space into grids that become denser all the time and, as divisibility advances, they seem to be refined indefinitely. Both the thought that governs the movements, and the movements themselves, are refined indefinitely by the increasing delicacy of sensations they unleash." While we normally perceive the direction of time through harmonic changes, such rhythmic tricks finally bring about the eradication of time. They bring to us music's timelessness. In the process, the sound is not devalued but soars beyond its boundaries.

Marie Jaëll's thought comes full circle. To achieve success, a performer must meet the technical and spiritual demands of the task. He must have, first of all, a clear musical conception of the piece he is going to play. Only then he can convey its spiritual essence, the truth underlying the notes. This approach is the gateway to transforming performance into an art.

The pianist perceives instantly the harmonic structure and the rhythmic patterns of the piece he is going to play. He senses its overarching melodies and goal-directed harmonics. Therefore, as he produces pure sounds, he balances them within a chord around the fundamental note. Then the melody comes in waves with its repetitive rhythms. In this way, conceptualization, hearing, and touch all cooperate in the interpretation of the melody.

Consequently, the resulting music evokes the motivational and emotional calls of the oriented movement. The resulting melodies let loose strong emotions, and emotions in their turn mobilize both the mind and the body.

---

114. Jaëll, M., Notebooks (Unpublished)

Music, of course, involves time in its very essence. But it is rhythmic, and the rhythmic periods melt into each other and blend. Thus is realized the ontological interrelation between time and rhythm. With this intertwining, time becomes suspended and remains almost motionless. As the rhythmic devices help eradicate time, music becomes a means of defeating time.

Music is sound, with a meaning it points to expressly beyond the sphere of the purely aesthetic: sound as something constant, thus a link with the permanent. Music is sound that defies time by going deep within. It gives access to the pure subject released from the world of objects and moving in obedience to the laws of freedom alone. Musical perception and its psychic impact belong to two different worlds. Beyond its physical confines, music becomes the bond that connects us to the unattainable and the eternal.

Unity on one side, boundlessness on the other — they are the two arches which sustain all work of art. This is exactly what Marie had perceived in the way Liszt played — the overall vision of the piece, on one side, and the multiple phrases and currents which run through it on the other.

We find everywhere in Marie Jaëll's work a search for unity and synthesis. The primeval unity is undifferentiated. She tries to disclose that unity through a conscious differentiation; and she achieves it by conflating time and space.

To Marie Jaëll, the profundity of music resides in the way that it offers access to the divine. All her pedagogy tries to realize Beethoven's ambition for music: "From the heart — may it speak to the heart." She enjoins the pianist to let his body vibrate with the intentionality of the music he is going to perform before he touches the keys. Her injunction is, "Be the music, before playing it."

Marie Jaëll's creative pedagogy soars to new heights as it transforms piano music's lack of continuity in sounds into a virtue, by giving value to the silence embedded in them. Her touch method thus becomes a gateway to the paradise of harmony. Music beyond its physical confines becomes that which connects us to the unattainable and the eternal.

Curiously, the paradise of harmony recalls the heaven of Buddhist god *Indra*. This great Buddhist god lords over a cosmos that is an infinite web of invisible lines and circles whose points of intersection are studded with shiny pearls. His divinity acts in such a way that in each pearl all the others are reflected, and in each reflection the infinite number of pearls is seen again. Indra's paradise is seen in each pearl, seen over and over again on a smaller and smaller scale. And devotees contemplate sound, to reach *nirvana*, which is infinite silence and which bathes the sounds of music.

Brahma's Cosmos

A Hindu myth recounts, "In the night of *Brahma*, when the universe was not yet created, matter was all inert. *Brahma* shook it from its torpor, and it began to quiver. Then *Brahma* entered the matter and gave it movement and rhythm. Time, Space, and Cause came to be."

This myth sums up Marie Jaëll's vision of art. Her view of music as movement directed by thought and as a channel of communion with other beings helped her discover its spatial and temporal dimensions, the dimensions that form the twin axes of the cosmos. From the vantage point of her musical aesthetics she enlarged her enquiry to the visual and plastic arts. She viewed architecture, sculpture, painting, and music as different manifestations of one Art. The phenomena that drive a composer to create a piece of music are also at work in a painter, a sculptor and an architect. Like all Romantics, she was haunted by the shimmering mirage of an ideal fusion of the arts.

Brahma is the model for all artists. Like him, they breathe time, space and movement into lifeless matter. What does a painter do before his canvas? In the space covering his view he perceives a moving set of diversely colored luminous spots where his eyes distinguish and recognize forms. Facing him is the surface, clear and inert, where nothing yet exists, longing for his magical touch. It docilely awaits his gestures as he imprints on it his thoughts, his message. Then it comes alive, totally transformed.

Kant viewed time and space as two innate human intuitions that trap man in contingency and decay. In such a view, the role of art would be to allow man to be stirred by the "intimations of immortality." Indeed, man is possessed by an urge to go beyond himself and to create works of art that conflate time and space so that he can transcend them. Truly, all works of art are "fragments of infinity." From Marie Jaëll's perspective, works of art are not a struggle to escape history but to live time and space fully. They are all intensified responses to the world, investing the ordinary with symbolic, supernatural significance.

She ranked artistic creations according to the idea they embody. "The more there is thought in art, be it in colors, stones or sounds, the greater that art is."[115] Looking at art as an artist, herself, she perceived a profound unity among all the arts.

Her approach is in stark contrast to Hegel's. In his "*Lectures on Aesthetics*," his discourse on art, he traces the development of the arts as a logical process accompanying and reflecting the unfolding of the "Idea."[116] He imposed a historical hierarchy among the arts. Egypt, home of the earliest civilization, specialized in architecture, the most materialist of the arts, and built pyramids in stone. Sculpture in marble reached its apogee in Greece; it was succeeded by the de-natured medium that is painting. As the "Idea" surged forward, less tangible arts like music and poetry entered the scene. Finally came Philosophy. Hegel was a philosopher and his views on art are colored by his nature.

Unfortunately, philosophers seem to be unreliable guides when it comes to the appreciation of arts. Plato had contempt for painting. Kant relegated music to the lower forms of pleasure. To him, music was just a simple game of sounds. Plotinus alone seems

---

115. Jaëll M., *Intelligence et Rythmes*, p.18
116. Gombrich

to have got it right, when he observed, "The form is not in the stone, it is in the designer before it enters the stone."

Incorporating her understanding of these philosophical views on art, Marie Jaëll built her aesthetics from her deeply lived experience of piano music. She started by subscribing to Hegel's view that the beauty of art is better and higher than the beauty of nature, because man-made art is an outpouring of the spirit. She also noted that the responses to beauty in art and to beauty in nature are interdependent, for what is beautiful in nature stimulates and deepens our sense of what is beautiful in art; and an artist illuminates things with his mind and projects their reflection upon other minds.

Above all, a work of art vibrates with emotional resonance that moves people. Its defining feature, according to Marie Jaëll, resides in its power to arouse us emotionally. Thus, it has a double function. First, it has a role as an image that is sensorial; second, it has a symbolic value, bearing a message. Thus, appreciating it requires the understanding of a particular culture at a definite moment of its history. Backed by such basic principles, Marie set out to explore the interlaced relationships among visual perception, knowledge and pictorial representation.

She spent long hours wandering about in museums. We can imagine her strolling around, stopping to contemplate at length the forms and colors of one painting, then of another, with her intense gaze. She knew how to sense their rhythms, composition and features as they unfolded themselves like ribbons in space before her eyes, and she could penetrate their inmost secrets.

She realized that the process of admiring art was primarily a mental activity. Indeed, an aesthetic theory becomes intelligible and profound only when it unearths the workings of the brain. She noted that as we look at a painting and fix on its different parts, our eyes are never immobile. They notice the multiple boundaries with oriented lines embedded in them, even if they are not perceptually explicit.

It occurred   to her that painting, sculpture and architecture express time in terms of space, in contrast to music — which lives in time and seeks space to burst forth. When we look at a painting, a piece of sculpture, or a monument, we first visualize it as a whole, and capture its spatial dimension. We are struck by its form, its innate, geometric design that gives it a bone structure. We perceive its details later and appreciate it at leisure by adding to it the time dimension.

In music, movement and rhythm help obliterate time. In visual arts, by contrast, real time is perceived in the "kinetic rhythm." The flow of lines and shapes in sculptures, paintings and monuments indicate time by both real and illusory movements. They express time that is neither static eternity nor monotonous regularity.

In her view, movements and rhythms bring a work of art to life as in Brahma's cosmos. As in music, the idea of movement is central to all forms of art. The rhythms underlying a work of art endow it with time, space, and structure.[117] The ultimate goal of an object of art is to create a fusion of space and time, and invite man to go beyond the contingency of his existence.

She started with painting. To her, painting (like all the arts) was a language. A painter's vocation would be to organize the elements that constitute that language. His thought first perceives something, and then decomposes it in order to recompose on the canvas, through his mastery of line and form. By controlling the movement, by sensing it in space, he gives form to his idea. He seeks to capture and fix the mutual relationships of objects in space, navigating like a seaman.

A painter communicates his rhythm by the contours of a line, by the rapidity of a stroke, which may easily be compared to the techniques used by pianists, the rapidity of an attack, of a motion. The living rhythm of a stroke, or of the phrasing, exists only if the artist foresees, and hears in advance, what he intends to express. The artist's thought is then projected outside where the perceptions

117. Gabo

of rhythm, of harmony, of movements take form. The work of art is a bridge that brings the inner and outer worlds together.

Marie's final research on painting and music was inspired by the analogy between the physical characteristics of light and sound. Both are waves, and both have spectra. During the last decades of the nineteenth century, psychologists showed that our experience of color and music are closely interwoven. Since then, artists have consciously exploited the affinities between music and color. Painters embrace light as their medium and geometric forms are their inspiration. They experience and depict space with quivering geometric figures.

Just as modern technology contributed crucial inputs to piano manufacture, modern industry and chemistry added stable anilines and abjarins to the painter's palette. Pre-Raphaelite painters, harking back to the Middle Ages, and the "back-to-nature" Impressionists, seized on the new opportunities offered by these manufactured pigments[118] and invented painting techniques that interleaved dabs of intense hue and the loosening of contour and brush strokes.

Baudelaire had remarked that it would be surprising if sound did not suggest color and if color did not evoke the idea of a melody. He wondered why no painter excelled in evolving spiritual space and depth, as Wagner did in music. The artists of the era compared the orchestra's instruments to different colors, and their tuning to setting up the palette. Then came Von Gogh, "a musician in colors" who spoke of the sonority of color. Wagner was his chief musical inspiration, and endowed his paintings with extravagance.

Marie Jaëll found that the language of movement that was so central to her aesthetics of music is also present in color. There is a continuity between the experiences of color in nature and in art, which explains why painting is so important to mankind. Moreover, the continuity with which lines in space or sounds in time follow each other is the natural symbol of the inner consistency of the

---

118. Ball, P. *Bright Earth : The Invention of Color*, Viking 2002

mind, and of the moral connection between action and emotion. Painting makes a synthesis of rhythmic forms and figures, and creates the effect of a choir among persons who compose the scene.

Directed movement thus becomes the centerpiece of Marie's aesthetics. It is a means to reach a goal, it is expressed by a stroke, a line, a curve, a motion...It guides the gaze to move around a picture, gives meaning to a sculpture, endows an edifice with equilibrium, helps play a musical phrase on the keyboard. It takes off from space, it has a direction, it lights up thought.

"Knowing how to draw," commented Delacroix, "means endowing the line with electricity that passes through it, and which, by induction, sends back an analogous echo to whoever looks at it."[119] A painter with his brush and a sculptor with his chisel make abstract ideas come to life, in color or in marble, through lines. They impart personally-inspired and emotionally-charged forms on inert matter.

Marie Jaëll noted that "a work coming out of one's hands is all the more perfect as a whole, the more all its components form the necessary inter-connections. It is typical of supreme artists to produce the greatest unity possible in their works, in such a way that the details not only do the least harm, but are of an absolute necessity there."[120]

She also made interesting observations on architecture, another art that concerned with space, light, movement and time. Space is most evident, since an architect's work is directly projected there. He must first technically master the unwieldiness and resistance of the materials he is going to use. He must compose with the physical volume and the play of forces involved. He has to relate details to the whole to present an overall vision. But the central building block is, after all, his thought that establishes equilibrium among the forces at work. It alone invests his creation with the

---

119.Diary, Delacroix.

120. Jaëll, M. *L'intelligence et le rythme*

sensation that he has triumphed harmoniously over unwieldiness and oppression by movement in space.

Thus architecture as art also seeks a balance of structural science and aesthetic expression. Its success depends on the essential mix of efficiency and delight. Every building presents a composition of masses, spaces, lines and colors. But it is an organic whole, and its inherent balance gives it beauty and strength. Its expressive style is a visual language. One could even say that a monument "performs" gracefully.

Curiously, architecture represents space as space-time. Temples, castles, cathedrals and pyramids express time *in terms of space*. They vibrate with intentionality and they are home to history dammed up and ghosts contained. If one sits amongst the stones and listens long and hard, one may catch echoes of praying monks, arrogant monarchs and toiling slaves. In the midst of silence, one can hear past voices whisper. A historic monument, as a piece of art, always conflates space and time.

A monument is recognition in stone, wood and brick of spiritual awakenings. It is a study of a building, accreting through time a coral reef of memories and desires. Architecture brings about a symbiosis of edifice and ritual.... A church makes a community for a space of time, then it disperses again.[121]

It is common to hear that "architecture is frozen music." In fact, the great monuments of humanity bristle with life. The great temples and cathedrals are brilliant examples of the organization of space within man-made confines of stone. Their constructions are carefully planned, a collaboration of symmetry and perspective. They are the repositories of humanity's memory and history. They teach us the continuity of tradition that is manifest in the sharing of values. If we sit still, and listen long and hard, we will hear voices of the past whispering to us.

---

121. Visser, M. *The Geometry of Love, Space, Time Mystery and Meaning in an Ordinary Church*, North Point Press

Continuing her research on the rhythm, Marie published another book in 1906: *Rhythms of the Gaze and Dissociation of Fingers*. After reading it, her friend Schuré sent the following letter:

Dear friend,

Thanks for sending me your interesting book on Rhythms of View and Dissociation of Fingers. Though written with perfect clarity and truly scientific precision, this book is not one of those that can be read at one stretch and absorbed in a day. One has to get used to your methods little by little, enter into your complex way of feeling and observing, learn to dissociate and coordinate one's sensations according to a new pattern. Then one realizes that, taking as a starting point your experience as a pianist, you have established the subtlest correlations among tactile, aural and visual sensations. All that is quite difficult, clearly, for a large majority of readers, but it is extremely suggestive to those who love to get to the bottom of things... It is easy to see, on putting together your several concordances, so delicately observed, that they tend to confirm the marvelous unity of human consciousness where touch, hearing and sight are only instruments of unity in the infinite. Thus thought Pythagoras, and so also Beethoven felt, no doubt, when he said, "Air is my kingdom; just as the wind whirls, my soul also whirls."

I wonder what your master Liszt would have said of this book, whose genius you define so well in your first pages, and whose creative interpretation has given you, so you say, a new memory, practically a new sense of harmony and music.

I think he would have approved and applauded. He would have admired the sharpness and perseverance with which you have pursued your curious investigations. He would have grasped it all, and taken it all in with one glance. He would have said, "I do not remember having thought all that, and above all I have reasoned like you do, but I have no doubt perceived it in my sub-consciousness and it must be true. God bless you, my girl, for you have discovered a new meaning... and maybe, you have created a new science while listening to the singing of the universal Word that speaks to you in rhythm and line.

As to me, I am not Liszt; I have some difficulty following you in detail. Yet, with a certain amount of effort, I do succeed. You have an analytical and auditory mind. I am synthetic and visual. In everything, I want seize the whole; I go forward, with head bent, in search of the cause and end, and at all cost, good or bad, right or wrong, I formulate them in a plastic image. In contrast, oh, how much wiser you are! You proceed by meticulous analysis, and observation of little facts. Thus you succeed in formulating laws which men of science will acknowledge, I imagine, and which will certainly be useful to artists. There is, however, a common ground where we bump into each other, I think: it is that of intuition and music. The intuitive and musical sense is one and the same thing for me, and is never separated, for it is the essence and the rhythm of all beings. That is why it is at the root itself of the plastic arts.

I have admired very much the application you make of it in Chapter IX on the visual and mental orientation in the arts. The double diagram you give of the master lines of the two *haut reliefs* of the Arc de Triomphe on the Champs Elysées is remarkable. In "Rude's departure," the harmony of main lines reveals at the first stroke the principal idea of the composition, the momentum of take-off that carries away the eye in its flight. On the other hand, in Cortot's triumph, the disharmony and dispersion of the lines ill expresses the idea of triumph, and lets it, so to say, fall into bits.

Your book ends with quite a pretty symbol of sparrows climbing the steps of a staircase, drawn by the image of an illusory pasture, and of leaves which descend, wafted by a light breeze. Well, you are the leaf that is swayed by the wind's rhythm, and I am the sparrow that hops from step to step dreaming of imaginary bits, but I forget them while gazing at the leaf in flight.

Cordial and sincere felicitations from your devoted
Ed. Schuré[122]

It is clear that Marie Jaëll was delving ever deeper in her research. The new book she published surprised, upset, even troubled some of her friends who felt that she was going too far, that she was venturing into obscure territory. Her intuitions seem to them obscure, and most of them could no longer follow her.

It is true that the book is a strange one for a musician to have written. In it, she studies the visual rhythms and their influence on the perception of the world that surrounds us. "One can consider the following research," she says, "as a series of visual exercises, meant not only to contribute to the perfecting of sight, but also of

122.BNUS, Schuré correspondance, Jaëll.

touch and hearing."[123] How far away we have traveled from the repetition of scales and other mechanical exercises!

Here, we are plunged into a sensory world where all our consciousness and sensibilities are caught up. The book offers visual exercises to be carried out by looking at different geometric figures and drawings. Depending on the character of the figures, the student is to hold his sight back, or carry it forward in his rhythm of movement; and Marie Jaëll offers observations of analogous impressions set in motion by works of art. Visual impressions can be classified into two categories: those that liberate the view and give life to the work, and those that impede it. These outer rhythms influence our inner rhythms more than one might imagine. The true meaning of rhythm is to give back life, to make things live, to give a soul, a meaning.

"A human being," she observed, "whose thought has acquired a more immediate and more intense inner movement, will also be able to perceive with greater intensity, through the movements of his gaze, the life that is on display before him: by this fact he will truly sense that he possesses the secret forces that animate him, and is more intimately bound to everything in nature that grows and stirs, is born and dies."[124]

During this part of her life, Marie found herself increasingly lonely. Charles Féré, who had become a close friend, was borne off prematurely in April, 1907. She was so distraught that she preferred not speak of her loss. Only a few touching lines, addressed to a friend, bear witness to the depth of her affection for him.

> If one day you meet a person who is driven by the same truth and who, by understanding what you carry within you, multiplies your abilities a hundredfold, in such a way as to make you believe that life has just begun, that all the past was nothing but the planting of a seed, you will find yourself so attached to him that

123. Jaëll, M. *Les Rythmes du Regard*, Introduction.
124. *Ibidem*

there is no other life but the one that originates there; from then on, everything derives from that, everything converges on it. Years may go by, but the union lives; it grows, every day brings a new blossoming. And after having been united right up until death, who can say that there would be any separation beyond the grave?

More than ever, she went her way, pursuing her course, untiringly seeking, and nothing could stop her in her research.

At this time, Marie was living on the fifth floor of a building on *rue Gay-Lussac*. She was so busy that she rarely left her apartment. Catherine Pozzi visited regularly and continued to work with her. Her diary speaks of her visits and shows what an impression Marie left on her visitors:

> There are five steep storeys to climb, with narrow steps, before ringing the bell at her apartment. And what do you see when the door opens? Beethoven's face, with the same high planes that make up his cheeks, his nose, his mouth, like a drawing by the same hand as the famous masque; two little gray eyes, lively and intense, a body that is muscular rather than heavy, that of a peasant more than a lady, of medium height but seemingly enlarged by a great natural dignity.
>
> She speaks softly, like all those who have respect for what they say. But when you play the piano before her, and badly, she starts screaming, with a surprising violence, and puts her hands all over yours, at the same time stretching them to stamp upon them the exact shape that is required, and the thunder from her mouth commanding all your faculties altogether she is a prophetess, formidable and powerful, inspired by God....[125]

So she taught a few students who still stayed with her, and she sometimes played concerts at home. All those who were lucky enough to hear her were greatly impressed by the quality of her playing. Several letters speak of it. One of her friends wrote to her:

> Dear Madame, The more I reflect, the more I try to come up with a clear vision of the crowd of impressions that overwhelmed

---

125. Kiener

me while you were playing, the more I feel that you have succeeded little by little in realizing the ideal instrument by which the divinity makes its laws known. Don't think I am speaking out of an enthusiasm that will lose in depth what spontaneity would gain. No, I am impressed very, very much by your playing and the incredible architectural harmony emanating from it; my mind reels, trying to find out where this impression comes from: a serenity that almost banishes emotion or, I should say, vulgar emotion from your playing. While I was listening to you, I had a very clear and almost tangible sense of the unity of all things.

The cosmic character — and the adjective signifies exactly what I feel — of the way you played overwhelms me. When the ear perceives the relations of tones that you render, problems of a nature entirely remote from music are clarified and are seen in a new light. What I heard at your place is like a crystallization of all the arts; and I would like to believe, as bizarre as it may seem, that art pursued this far, that is to say beyond oneself, would in the end make us understand, or would give birth to, a new conception of the Universe. It's not clear to me yet, but there is a truth here, in any case — and it shines forth, dazzling; your existence is more necessary than ever to the poor seekers of the Infinite. So I wish you a long life, at this start of the year.

Yours,

M. Ritséma Van Eck.[126]

Yet Marie Jaëll was still not satisfied with her results; she was in fast forward, and her work was constantly evolving. It became very hard for her friends to keep up with her...More and more she found herself alone.

In addition, her character turned sharply uncompromising and authoritarian. She had a despotic streak in her that could, in a fit of anger, break the closest ties.

As always, she was totally indifferent to success. "Success, like money, sounds hollow," she would say. She never did make the least concession in order to succeed, and every day that God gave her she put to use at her research. Her method, relatively simple at first,

---

126.Ibidem

became more and more enriched as she explored, discovered, and wrote. Few indeed could keep up!

Most of her musician friends thought she was taking things too far, and little by little they distanced themselves from her. Her challenge to traditional methods of teaching and her questions on musical aesthetics were intimidating.

Scientists, however, monitored her research with interest. She received quite abundant correspondence from many of them. Here are some extracts:

Madame,
Your thinking is surprisingly penetrating and suggestive. It is because he has hands, the Greeks used to say, that man is the most intelligent of animals. Even more, Minerva would lose her wisdom if she lost her hands.

You regret that most people do not think with both their hands at the same time; how many are there, even among those who pass for cultured, who are not capable of thinking even with a single hand! Like you, I am convinced that most of the men of our epoch prefer to let their motor images atrophy in favor of the all-powerful and invading visual image...

I am not a musician, but I have been singularly attracted by the psychophysics and psychology of music which you ceaselessly advance with such inventive wealth and ingenuity. How I wish I had the time to follow in your steps, experimenting and analyzing for myself the correlations and evocations you indicate. What a pity not to have every day a triple measure of time — one could easily fill it with beautiful, curious or useful things !...

A.Lalande[127]

Another wrote:

Madame,
I have read your manuscript with the greatest interest. These explorations testify to your rare capacities of observation and exceptionally refined sensual sensitiveness.

127.BNUS Letter from Lalande to Jaëll.

In nature, everything counts, and our organism does not escape that law; everything in it is bound together in a sovereign harmony, and the vocation of science is to disclose its chords...
     E. Coustet[128]

Scientists often write to her, responding to her articles or to her books. One of them, a doctor and researcher, wrote to her:

> The question of the scientific and experimental definition of artistic beauty is surely tempting. I have had occasion to reflect on the matter many times, and I deem it to be one of the hardest questions to deal with. Art is the intuitive expression of numerical relations that exist among the vibrations of different natures that impress on our senses. The Ancients used to say that God acts geometrically.

Marie Jaëll was, at bottom, discoursing on how one should appreciate a work of art. Her pedagogy teaches us how to refine our sensory, visual and aural perceptions. Its objective is to let us glimpse the unity between the inner and outer worlds, and recover Brahma's cosmos enlivened by time, space and movement so that "art teaches us not only see and listen but also to be. It makes us what we are."

An aesthetic experience, in her view, always involves a focus. It is highly directional and does not occur in a casual manner. It is a profound dialogue that leads to the forgetting of the self. The world of sound, light and silence can only be experienced in the depth of one's being. As Matisse said, seeing is already a creative process in search of the essential, and to put order into color relationships is to put order into our ideas. In sum, the true meaning of art is in the mind of the viewer who looks at an object of art.

Jaëll began with music, of course, the domain she knew best. Hearing music, one may note, is a passive process — by contrast, listening to music is a creative and active engagement, comparable to following a speech. We hear both, sound by sound. What retains our attention is the idea underlying the flow of words and notes.

128.Lalande

Automatically we link together certain familiar groups of words or notes. We are conscious that the reality of the speech or music is not located in the discursive concatenation of notes or verbal elements but can be found in the interstices and in the aggregation of sounds and agreements. Listening to music thus must be based on the principles of perception and aesthetics.

In contrast to paintings, sculptures, books or poems that remain essentially the same, music has its life rekindled with every performance. This capacity for permanent renewal is one of the wonders of music. The interpreter breathes life into the musical partition by constant gradation, shading of tone, and subtleties of timing. Thanks to the beauty and vibrancy of the sounds he produces, he transmits the feeling of deep involvement and transports his listeners into a world of magic and mystery.

Music listening is not story-centered but music-centered. A performer needs to create a dialogue at the piano, without saying a word, and engage with his listeners. Then the listener perceives music as more than a sequence of notes with different pitches and duration. In the words of Stravinsky, "We could best appreciate the sensation produced by music only by identifying it with the emotion which the contemplation of the play of architectural forms arouses in us."

"A painting gets its unity from the way it is drawn, and a piece of music reveals its unity in the manner it is played. The overall composition has value only when all its visible, and even invisible, parts are bound by an indissoluble empathy. No fragment of its parts can be separated, or even modified, without the whole suffering a counter-shock. The global appreciation of a painting or of a partition is made as soon as the thought, after having visualized the whole, is able to discern the details, the minutest plans, to analyze the play of forms, of harmonies, in order to restore them in their pristine unity. Only then does a work of art take on true meaning as one looks at it, listens to it, plays it." Marie Jaëll could subscribe entirely to Van Gogh's wish (expressed in a letter to his sister in 1886) that his paintings would be witnessed by an audience the way a violin or piano concert is taken in.

To the Romantics, paintings are windows on the world; they are recordings of colored sensation. They become another word for feeling. The viewer is invited in; the painting instantly initiates a visual dialogue with the viewer. Eventually, the viewer "rediscovers" the painter's thought on the canvas. It is a dynamic act to perceive the relationships of lines and colors of a painting. We explore them with our gaze. We focus on one area and fix our orientation in order to discover the resolution and the palette of colors. The line that was traced by the artist, we, in our turn, retrace, seeking to follow its course and thus to restore to it its initial movement, its life. As the viewer looks at a painting and fixates its different parts, his eyes are never totally immobile. We reach a full understanding of a painting when we capture the rhythms of forms and figures that project a stunning image of unity in contrast.

While admiring a painting, the eye takes delight in following the course of curves which advance and alternate, and which conjure up a visual dance. Hogarth, in his treatise "The Analysis of Beauty," singles out the influences the play of lines can have on vision. "An appealing movement gives me the same kind of sensation that I happen to feel on seeing a country dance."

Marcel Duchamp began to produce paintings that suggest movements statically. In painting, there is a concern to fix the mutual relations of two objects in space, a balancing act which the painter approaches with delicacy and finesse.

Painting may express that which is; music purports a becoming. Art becomes a means of defeating time. The conflation of time and space is achieved through intentionality that permeates them and gives them unity. Painting and architecture depend on space; music depends on time. It is a magical time-machine enabling us to vibrate with the thoughts and emotions of people who may be long gone.

Works of art bring us into communion with another human being. That communion as created via the world of silence and sound can best be experienced in the concert hall. This explains the extreme attentiveness of audiences at concerts of classical music. The feats of concentration and stillness on the part of listeners as well as performers recall religiously ordered events.

The intense and living sensoriality Marie developed helped her feel and perceive refined relations among the different human senses. She could now penetrate the truly subtle domains of consciousness. Studying for hours the immense hand of Rudé's statue "Victory," then at the Trocadero, she got the idea of associating colored sensations to the sensitivity of each finger. String players were already very conscious that the tactility of color could be matched by a tactility of sound. To her, color was a supplementary means to help refine tactile sensations. Perhaps each finger could be felt in correlation with a color of the solar spectrum, and be filled with the quality proper to that color.

Thus she wrote her next book, published in 1910: *A New State of Consciousness: Coloring of Tactile Sensations.* She says in the preface,

> I must admit that, in seeking a solution to the problem of the harmony of touch, I have an objective other than that of musical education. When the harmony of touch, such as I conceive it, is applied to the teaching of music, we are dealing not only with the efficiency of the musicality of thought but also with the develop- ment of intelligence.
>
> Our hands are called upon to feel certain vibratory relations whose existence has been ignored till now. In whatever measure the definition of these relations is grasped, one will be persuaded that the search for beauty has value only when it coincides with that of beauty. Quite a new influence can intervene in the training of the hand: I want to speak about the influence of colors. My research on musical touch has in fact led me to note not only that the sensitiveness of the fingers is exalted as soon as one assigns to each of them an appropriate color, but that the static and dynamic activity of the hand is strengthened.[129]

---

129. Jaëll, M., *Un nouvel état de conscience*

The influence of colors on the musicality of piano playing is multi-faceted. They contribute powerfully to the differentiation of sensations. Marie Jaëll compared the awakening of the hand's sensibility to a plant that, after a more or less prolonged period of inertness, comes back to life, and blooms.

"The sensitivity of my hand seemed to me for the first time comparable to a language whose meaning I could grasp."[130] Here, Marie Jaëll was venturing into a subtle world, indeed. She had achieved such a degree of sensitivity that very few of her pupils could follow her in her path.

In an article on Marie Jaëll, Catherine Pozzi asks:

> Is there any need to say that, to succeed in establishing these infinitely delicate concordances, required nothing less than the surprising organization of precision and refinement of this great artist who is an experimentalist of the highest order? The scale of equivalent values between tactile sensations and color sensations is impossible to control for a non-refined hand; but is accessible without exception to all those who have developed their touch through intelligent study... It is strangely simple that in the different impressions given by the contacts of the fingers — thumb, middle finger, ring finger,...; there are exactly the same ratios of the five colors of a prism...

"...But all these things are hidden from us," Marie Jaëll concludes her book. "Maybe that is how our thoughts are born through innumerable ways whose mutual differences escape us."

Marie Jaëll pursued her research in this minute and delicate domain of sensation and published her last important book in 1912, *The Resonance of Touch and Topography of the Fingertips.*

This book is a continuation of her investigations, and in it she explores indefatigably the infinite world of the hand's sensitivity in relation to colors, of musical touch, of listening, of resonance. Increasingly withdrawn from the world, she worked (often at night, as her diary reveals) and sometimes, in the early hours of the

---

130.Ibidem

morning, she would stroll along the boulevards or walkways along the quays, her eyes filled with the intensity of the fire that burned within her. From discovery to discovery, she soared to heights where air is rare.

"When all the strings of the body can no longer stand the tension," she wrote, "I cannot live any more in the open air. The atmosphere of the days of study is so feverish that my joy consumes me, and then I need some ordinary hours to recover. Banality is a solace to me."[131]

THE DECLINING YEARS

We arrive at the year 1914. Once again, war is tearing Europe apart. German armies march on Paris. Marie leaves her beloved city with one of her pupils. When the menace fades, she returns home. The events of the Great War remind her of the sufferings caused by the war of 1870, and for a second time in her life the fate of her homeland Alsace is at stake. "I hope terribly," she exclaims; "I never stop thinking about having our homeland returned to us. For so long, we have been looking at it from here as if we wanted to draw it towards us by the sheer force of our desires."[132]

In 1918, she left *rue Tournon* and set up housekeeping in *Avenue de la Muette* at Passy. For one last time she returned to Alsace; then she went back to Paris, where she stayed for the rest of her life.

Her new apartment was on the seventh floor. Ignoring the elevator, she would walk up and down the stairs without showing the least signs of fatigue. Near her apartment, in the loft, was a workroom, home to a large piano. She would work there in the light that filtered through a stained glass window. When she was not playing, a mysterious silence filled the loft Odd pieces of furniture lined the walls, but there was nothing to attract the attention. From

---

131. Jaëll, M., Diary
132. Letter to her nephew Fritz Kiener

the top of a gallery a French tricolor flag hung down in large folds, a gift from her pupils on Victory Day. Liszt's portrait was displayed in the position of honor, above the piano.

The workroom commanded an enchanting view of Paris. A vast horizon unfolded before the windows, revealing the city's scintillating charms under the changing light as day shifted to evening.

Marie spent the last years of her life there, solitary, but crowded with the world that she had discovered and invented. "My art, which is a science, has come to life as the full flowering of all the struggles of my past life. I would like to cry, cry all day in thanksgiving for having been guided by a true blessing till the end of my work. And it seems to me that I could never cry enough to express the full measure of the gratitude that I bear in all my being."

Marie vibrated with a thrilling sensibility that made her feel life's joys and pains with equal intensity. Yet she knew the bitterness of solitude, the inner solitude of those who step away from the known pathways to risk unexplored directions, in search not of success but of truth.

There is no doubt that in the evening of her life she missed the sense of approval her work once had enjoyed. She was nostalgic for it. She could do without success, but she did have a heart-felt need to be understood. "I beg you," she implored her nephew, "only put a word on paper and drop it in an envelope, a word to tell me, yes, I have read; it will do me so much good. Your letter made me feel happy that I am thinking in unison with another one. I am so starved for such fellow feeling....And it makes my work harder, drier..."

She was fortunate to still have a few rare but true friends and pupils around her. She instructed them on her latest discoveries and communicated her enthusiasm to them without respite. But she did not receive anybody else. If by chance some visitor, known or otherwise, knocked at her door in the hope of meeting her, she immediately slammed it shut, saying: "Madame Jaëll? No, this is not her address."

Among her most loyal friends, André Siegfried and Maurice Pottecher would sometimes hole themselves up with her for a get-together. In an article for the journal, *Le Monde Français*, Siegfried talks about his last visits to Marie Jaëll:

> I see her vast workroom in Passy, again, where she lived the life of a recluse... The musician herself opened the door and welcomed me. On the spot she shared with me her most recent research and her latest discoveries, in a soft and mysterious voice, with the faith of a believer and the simplicity of a child. I listened to her in silence, cradled by her words, both touched by the boldness of her genius and vaguely anxious about the unknown horizons towards which she was dragging me. Sometimes she would finish by sitting at the keyboard: a heavy form, ageless, evoking both old age and the youthful eternity of Sybille, inclining her powerful brow. Her half-closed eyes would suddenly light up to let the flash of a lightening look pass through the slit of her eyelids. Under her hands, wonderful hands, the hands of a twenty-year-old, moving in rhythmic swings, harmonies slipped through, at times slow and lithe, at the utmost limit of perception, at other times precipitating like cascades and dripping with sounds...

Often on Sunday mornings Marie played for her pupils and friends. None of them could forget the atmosphere of the place, and the music that was extraordinarily buoyant, with quasi-immaterial, wonderfully powerful sonorities elicited by her unique hands.

Maurice Pottecher, deeply impressed by her personality, reflected,

> However strong the differences of minds, epochs and arts, I cannot help noticing an analogy between the scientific presentiments contained in Marie Jaëll's books and those whose secrets are revealed in the notebooks of Leonardo da Vinci. A novel, intuitive and thoughtful conception of the universe leaps out in a mixture of precision and obscurity, demonstrable truths and bold hypotheses, always with a somewhat rash or naive aspect to them. The figure of this remarkable person, who exercised an irresistible influence on a small number of those who were close to her, is not unworthy, whatever be her destiny, of comparison with one of the

greatest minds of the Renaissance. Similar mindsets may not end up obtaining the same rank of glory. To this (that is to say, to glory), Marie Jaëll remained indifferent, or at least to success — a great sacrifice for a mind for which nothing burns feebly, even pride and ambition. She lived as an ascetic, "true to herself" as she would say, devoured by the thirst for progress, both heart and mind consumed for a God in whom were fused Beauty and Bounty, aesthetic and moral perfection and extension of Knowledge without end.[133]

In spite of her abundant and rich accomplishments, she did pine after a fuller life:

> Oh, grief without end! In each of us there is a being other than the one that we see. All our aspiration forms the image of what we ought to be. Certainly the elaboration of this image has value, and we should take note of it. But the best part of us stays locked up within us because we do not find the right form to incarnate it. How does it happen that we do not make efforts to relate to this inner flame, and remain in relation only with the being which moves and acts on the outside?[134]

To the end of her life Marie Jaëll remained alert, always on the move, and ready to listen. Her mind did not cease for a moment to observe. She remained contemplative, and welcomed with emotion the revelations life offered her. By becoming aware of the subtle worlds that surrounded her, she learned to understand better the human being — what is most beautiful and good in him.

She seemed so distant from others; yet she seemed to know them better than anybody else, and she loved them with a true love which only those who go beyond themselves possess.

She took great delight in strolling in the gardens. To her, nature was a continuous source of inspiration. As soon as she returned home from her walks, she would unburden her inner

---

133. Quoted in Kiener pp 103-104
134. Jaëll, M. Notebooks, unpublished

impressions in her notebooks, pages covered with her beautiful handwriting, big, strong, and accented.

This Sunday, May 16, I went for a walk in the Luxembourg gardens in the company of a gentle west wind that transformed all the trees there into musicians. I enjoyed looking at them and listening to their music. I watched the slightly jerky and curtailed swinging of clipped orange trees in their tubs, the light and elegant rhythm of the pomegranates, the altogether different swaying of palm tress with short or long leaves, the rhythmic poverty of the monotonic to-and-fro waving of the lilacs, the rhythmic heaviness of hawthorns with overgrown branches that blocked the path to the wind puffs, and the extraordinary rhythmic grace of the tress with long branches..."[135]

Other pages reveal the depth and originality of her vision of the world. She let herself be permeated with all the flavors of life. And then she would turn them into matter for reflection.

While walking one day, I saw a flock of birds in distress (frightened no doubt by some unusual cause) swoop down on a fir tree near by. Uttering cries of fear while lining up on its branches, they seemed to set the whole tree vibrating. I was listening to this tumultuous orchestra when, with a single stroke of wings, they all fled.

Once they had disappeared, another sound filled the space. This time it was a group of children, already big and vigorous; shouting, they impetuously rushed up to the same fir tree, and went beyond it and vanished. What a contrast between the cries that expressed the great distress of the birds and the vibrant and screaming noises of this flock of children moving in the same direction!

The continuity of these infinitely changing clamors is a poignant gratitude to the emotions that are contained in those voices! It is there that we find the true human music, the music without notation! It is, no doubt, the most beautiful music, for in the incandescence of life manifested by these young beings, we sense the affirmation of eternal truths, of the secret harmony of communi-

---

135. *Ibidem*

ties. Before the unutterable greatness of this intuitive polyphony we feel we are in the presence of the primordial source, from which all artistic manifestations spring. The clamor of the children lives on in my thought as an apotheosis of the human voice! It must be noted that among musicians only those who possess this deeply emotional survival of resonance can evoke musical beauty.[136]

Marie filled page after page of her notebooks with equally intense emotion. She jotted down her thoughts and ideas, the fruit of her reflections, the outcome of one experience or another, and started afresh the following day and commented once more. She unveiled the hidden analogies of the sensitivities of the hand with the aural and visual senses that link humans to the world that surrounds them. In her journals, more than in the books intended for the general public — where she mainly wished to present herself as a scientist — she revealed herself as a poet, philosopher and deep mystic.

...My art, to what heights it takes me soaring...

...This force of progress, from where does it spring?

...As the planetary systems form and dissolve, we see, in our awareness of touch, combinations of sensations forming and dissolving themselves. The former, thanks to their duration, hint at the idea of the infinite; the latter evolve in a few seconds, and nonetheless form an essential element of our thought. Viewed from this angle our thought reflects the continuous image of the evolution of the universe. The domain of thought is animated by the same laws that govern matter in the visible space.

In the later days of her life, her memories of Liszt became more intense. Absent but ever present, he had guided her and helped her bring out her hidden talents. In her thoughts, he was her constant companion.

---

136. *Ibidem*

When I see a glimpse of the splendors of dissociation, I cannot but help thinking of Liszt. This evening I played the third Mephisto waltz that seemed to me prodigiously intense...I don't think I have played it in the last twenty-five years. If only I could have played this way for Liszt! The joy he would have had on listening to this music, which is his and mine.

...This morning I experienced something fantastically beautiful while playing "La Ronde des Gnomes." I felt Liszt was next to me at the piano, as if we were playing it together — he through his spirit, me with my hands infused by the same spirit.

In the evening of February 4, 1925 Marie Jaëll quietly passed away. Her last words were, "I still have so much to do!" This was her last prayer; all her life she had looked upon work as prayer, following the Benedictine ideal, *laborare est orare*. With the passage of time, her work has taken on a new dimension and a reality that outlived her; the work lives for all time.

Her pupils and the rare friends who had stood by her paid her a last homage. They took the flag down from the gallery, imbued as it was with the marvelous essence of her music, and wrapped her body in it.

Epilogue

Viewed with a century's hindsight, Marie Jaëll's accomplishments seem extraordinary. She was a pioneer in piano pedagogy and a path-setter in musical aesthetics. Her phrase "touch the piano" — in the sense she gave it — is now part of piano folklore. Pianist Charles Rosen claimed that "what interested him most of all in the experience of playing the piano was the relation of the physical act of playing to those aspects of music generally considered more intellectual, spiritual and emotional;"[137] this is a faithful echo of her view of playing the piano. Yet hers is an unfamiliar name in the history of piano music; it would seem that her achievements were shortchanged by time.

The nineteenth century was hard on women. Its bourgeois culture preferred to see them as charming ornaments, to be seen but not heard. It decreed that they embodied the mundane, and stick to their knitting. However, "the more we know about what women have achieved in the past, the more reason we have to wonder why their achievements have been so frequently forgotten in the present."[138]

137.Winter R., "Piano Man," *The New York Review of Books*, October 23, 2003

It is true, she was a Romantic, and Romanticism "marked the return of the repressed." Still, it was elitist and ambiguous in its attitude towards women, and in the main it excluded them from public life. Fortunately, it also created an intellectual space for them, even if it kept them out of the institutions of higher learning.[139]

The world of music was still less receptive to women. As Rosen observes, "the few women composers, whose work remained almost completely repressed during the time, were harshly excluded from history."[140] Most critics writing about Marie Jaëll's music showered her with left-handed compliments, speaking of the manliness of her compositions.

Marie Jaëll was not born to high culture, and she had no positive role model to emulate. She found her own bearings and followed a path of her own. Her achievements stemmed in large part from her moral stamina. She trusted her impulses; she possessed exceptional gifts of insight and understanding. Her senses never dulled or dimmed by the constant familiarity with her beloved instrument, she invented a fresh approach to piano pedagogy and pursued it with unflagging energy.

In an unassuming way, she personally experienced the great scientific revolution that was overtaking Europe during her lifetime. She was convinced that her art was at the same time a science. She had a true scientific calling and all her work is founded on mutually self-sustaining theory and experimentation. Lacking today's techniques, borrowed from computer science, she turned to thought experiments as an investigative tool. Then, relying heavily on the intuitions of her own penetrating mind, she managed to isolate the variables in order to simulate piano sounds and trace the causes of minute differentiations.

---

138. Redusen, JE. *Sexual Politics in Comte and Durkheim*: Feminism, History and the French Sociological Tradition, *Signs* Autumn 2001 : 229-264

139. Rosenblum, Nancy L. *Another Liberalism*, Harvard University Press 1987 p.2

140.Rosen, C. *The Romantic Generation*, Harpers Collins Publishers p XI

Unsurprisingly, Marie Jaëll's aesthetics echo the views of mathematicians on their chosen subject. For example, Hermann Weyl argues that the task of mathematics is to grasp continuity, given by intention, in the flow of time and motion as a totality of discrete stages. To him, mathematics is an attempt to understand the natural continuum in terms of the discrete which is its very opposite. Marie Jaëll sought to concatenate discrete musical sounds into continuous and rhythmic patterns. Indeed, both music and mathematics are about seeing relationships from two opposite viewpoints.

In spirit, Marie Jaëll was close to quantum physicists, who may talk like mystics, and speak of conflating space and time, or declare that lines and dots (or waves and particles, in their jargon) can be perceived to be the same. Heisenberg, the founder of quantum physics, observes, "When we speak of the picture of nature in the exact science of our age, we do not mean a picture of nature so much as a picture of our relationship with nature."[141] But "neither biology nor quantum theory dictates the nature of the relational realm."[142] Marie Jaëll, as an artist, started from the relational realm and to understand it turned to science.

The union between art and science that Marie Jaëll realized in her life would be the envy of C.P. Snow, a British scientist turned novelist. He regretted that science and art were two cultures that did not understand and trust each other. Marie Jaëll succeeded in turning to science to get a better grasp of her art.

In a century whose leitmotif was rationality, she developed a clear philosophy of music to back up her teaching. Indeed, in pedagogy, she was abreast, if not ahead, of her times. At its core she put consciousness. A philosopher notes, "Future generations will wonder why it took us so long in the twentieth century to see the centrality of consciousness in the understanding of our very existence as human beings."[143] She sensed the ontological affinity of

---

141. Heisenberg, W., *La Nature dans la Physique Contemporaine*, Gallimard, 1962, p.33.

142. Hoffman, D.D. *Visual Intelligence*, p. 199

consciousness and sound, and noted that both sound and conscious states require time for their existence, without requiring its extension. In her view, the consciousness finds in sound an image of itself. Out of that intuition evolved her conviction that consciousness must play a central role in piano teaching. She relentlessly defended the idea that what distinguishes great piano playing is not the technique *per se* but the sheer intelligence of the interpretation.

Her phrase, "directed movement," sums up her vision of music — indeed, of all art. Such an idea was trendy for the epoch; the idea of movement, as a component of works of art, began to ferment in other artists' minds during the period from 1910 to 1920.[144]

In her view, touch depends on movement as vision depends on light. "Sound is the medium for the transport of directed movement that is music," she would say.

In the last few decades, knowledge of the human brain and its cognitive function has made spectacular progress. *Nature* magazine made the claim in 2002 that "Neuro-scientists are starting to discover how our brains process music."[145] They find that the emotional response to music is processed in a set of structures distributed widely through the brain. They also add that making music requires well-honed motor skills and relies on a high level of integration between auditory inputs and muscle control. Attempts are being made to reach a better understanding of music's role in human existence. But, in spite of all the experts' efforts, it is likely that music will always remain an enigma to neurobiologists.

Marie Jaëll was faithful to the European tradition in Western music that emphasizes a relaxed approach for the realization of musical sound. In particular, she always adopted a rather flexible attitude with regard to the actual pitch content of a composition. She was convinced that every performance of piano music was a

---

143. Searle
144. Gabo
145. *Nature*, March 7, 2002 p.12-14

creation and as such was unique. The written text springs to life in the tactile, aural, visual, intellectual, and above all, emotional experience of the pianist.

She followed closely the late nineteenth century psychology, which took note of the analogy between color and music. Already, string players were highly conscious that the tactility of color could be matched by the tactility of sound. Unfortunately, this is on direction where her research could have gone farther.

In many ways Marie Jaëll resembles Maria Montessori, the first woman to qualify as a doctor (in 1896) from an Italian university. She also advocated a systematic education of the senses. Both women pioneered pedagogical methods that insisted on teaching children spatial awareness through the touch.

Another pedagogue close in spirit to Marie Jaëll was Jean Piaget, the Swiss psychologist, who likened children to little scientists. Both realized that scientists and children are similar since both avidly try to make sense of the world. By unraveling the deep links between aural art and the brain, Marie Jaëll showed that a major function of art is to enlarge the brain's capacity to seek knowledge about the world. Her analysis of the unconscious was motivated by her ambition to bring into the open the hidden capacities that had been accumulating for millennia in the human brain.

Marie Jaëll believed that "art teaches us not only to see and hear, but also to be. It makes us what we are." An artist is neither a historian nor a prophet. He is a simple explorer of existence. His art is the expression of his personal vision that has a cosmic reach. Music in particular moves us in the depth of our being and enriches our emotional experience. Its power lies in the way it works upon our feelings rather than in the way it works upon our thoughts. And, its resources are limitless. "It is a vast river, and one may dip into its waters at any point and come out refreshed."

Marie Jaëll's approach to music showed that industrial capitalism, flourishing on a large scale during her lifetime, could not obliterate the human desire to escape the confines of the ego. She was not concerned with music's tendency to promote coherence within social groups; she saw in music a gift from God — a sense of eternity, and with it an idea of the fulfillment of our desire for peace and harmony.

To Marie Jaëll, music was a mystery. And when we face a mystery, we can only stare in wonder and bewilderment, not knowing what explanations would even look like. We can only glimpse that it is the deepest act of man's creativity to make contact with the universe and the divine. Through vigilant attention to the sensual world and through fidelity to the spirit, we can hope to reach some understanding of music's power and beauty. Her aesthetics grew out of a deeply religious classical and humanist view of art.

For all the bafflement with which Marie Jaëll's results were received, her words are now remembered; and pianists are learning to hear them and value them. Her passion for her art led her to probe the relationship between the inner and outer worlds that constitute human life and culture. At the sanctified core of music, Marie Jaëll found a beam of light to guide mankind from the outer world to the inner realm of divine mystery.

Bibliography

I. Works by Marie Jaëll

a. Books

La Musique et la Psychophysiologie (1896), Editions Alcan, Paris

Le Mécanisme du Toucher (1897), Editions Colin, Paris

Le Toucher, L'Enseignement du Piano Basé sur la Physiologie (1899)

L'Intelligence et le Rythme dans les Mouvements Artistiques (1904) Editions Alcan, Paris

Les Rythmes du Regard et la Dissociation des Doigts (1906), Editions Fischerbacher, Paris

Un Nouvel Etat de Conscience: La Coloration des Sensations Tactiles (1910), Editions Alcan, Paris

La Résonance du Toucher et la Topographie des Pulpes (1912), Editions Alcan Paris

Nouvel Enseignement Musical et Manuel Basé sur la Découverte des Boussoles Tonales (1922) Les Presses Universitaires.

b. Commentaries and Reports

Commentary on Liszt's Works, on the occasion of concert programs given in Salle Pleyel, edited in 1891, Editions Chaix

La Grande Œuvre de l'Education de la Main, A Report to the Congress of the French Association for the Advancement of Science, July 26, 1920 Stratsbourg, edited in 1921, Editions Chaix

Two books made up of extracts from Marie Jaëll's work:

Le Toucher musical par l'Education de la main, Extracts from six books of Marie Jaëll, by Mme J. Culmann, 1922, Les Presses Universitaires

La Main et la Pensée musicale, texts compiled in 1927 by Marie Jaëll's disciples, with a preface by André Siegfried, Les Presses Universitaires

Diary: Marie Jaëll's working diary consists of 32 handwritten notebooks.

c. Musical Compositions

Marie Jaëll composed approximately 80 musical pieces, most of which were published during her lifetime:

Impromptu

Deux Méditations

Six Petits Morceaux à Marie Claire

Sonate (dedicated to Liszt)

Dix Bagatelles (dedicated to H. Herz)

Esquisses Romantiques

Feuillet d'album

Six valses mignonnes

Six valses mélancholiques

Sphinx

Prisme (dedicated to Saint-Saëns

Promenade matinale

Les beaux jours

Les jours pluvieux

Ce qu'on entend dans l'Enfer

Ce qu'on entend dans le Purgatoire

Ce qu'on entend dans le Paradis

Valses à quatre mains

Les Voix du Printemps

Piano d'accompagnement de Marie Jaëll des Vingt Pièces pour le piano, op. 58 de Banjamin Godard

Concerto en ut mineur

II. OTHER WORKS

a. Articles

Bosch van's Gravemoer, J., "L'Oeuvre de Marie Jaëll," *Le Monde musical*, April 1925.

Capgras J., Marie Jaëll, "Un nouvel état de conscience," *Revue générale des sciences*, 28 Feb. 1981

Chevalier L., "Deux méthodes d'enseignement psychophysiologique de Marie Jaëll à Youry Bilstin," *Le monde musical*, 30 Sept. 1927

J.B., "La Secrétaire de Liszt : Marie Jaëll," *Mercure de France*, 15 June 1928

J.-D. B., "La Résonance du Toucher et la Topographie des Pulpes, par Marie Jaëll," *Journal de Psychologie*, 1913.

Laloy, L., "Marie-Jaëll," *Revue Musicale*, May 1925

Pottecher, M., "Marie Jaëll," *le Monde français*, Dec. 1948

Pottecher, M., "Une Amie de Liszt : Mme Marie Jaëll," *Sup. Littéraire du Figaro*, 4 Dec. 1926

Pozzi-Bourdet C., "Le Problème de la Beauté musicale, l'œuvre de Marie Jaëll," *Cahiers Alsaciens*, Strasbourg, March 1914 *b. Books*

Abraham, G., *The Age of Beethoven 1790-1830*, Oxford 1985

Askenfeldt, A., *Five Lectures on the Acoustics of the Piano*, Royal Institute of Technology, Stockholm. 1988.

Askenfeldt, A. and Jansson E.V., "From Touch to String Vibrations," I II III IV and V, *Journal of the Acoustical Society of America*

Berlin, I. *The Roots of Romanticism*, (ed by H. Hardy) Princeton University Press 1999

Berlin, I., "Counter-Enlightenment," *Dictionary of the History of Ideas*, Charles Scribner's Sons. New York, 1972

Bilson, M., "The Viennese Fortepiano of the late 18th century," *Early Music*, April 1980

Brinlmann, R., "In the Times of the 'Eroica'," in *Beethoven and His World*, Burnham S. and Steinberg M.P. (ed.), Princeton University Press

Brookner, A., *Romanticism and Its Discontents*, Farrar, Straus and Giroux

Changeux, Jean-Pierre. *Raison et Plaisir*, Odile Jacob, 2002

Chantavoine, Félix, *Liszt*, Alcan

Closson, Ernest. *History of the Piano*. Translated by Delano Ames; edited and revised
by Robin Golding. Scholarly Press. 1947

Colt, C.F., "Early Piano," *Early Music*, January 1973

Dart Thompson, *The Interpretation of Music*, Hutchinson London, 1967

Ehrlich, C. *The Piano, A History*, J.M. Dent and Sons, London, 1976

Einstein, A., *Romanticism in Music*.

Elderan, G.M. and Tonori G., *Comment la Matière Devient la Scène*, Odile Jacob, 2000

Franklin, R., "Good Vibrations," review of S. Isacoff's book *Temperament, The Idea that Solved Music's Greatest Riddle*, in *The New Republic*, December 13, 2001

Fuster, J. M., *Memory in the Cerebral Cortex*, MIT Press 1999

Georgiadis T., *Music and Language* (translated by Gollner M.L). Cambridge University Press 1982

Goebl W., *Skilled Piano Performance: Melody Lead caused by Dynamic Differentiation*, Austrian Research Institute for Artificial Intelligence Vienna

Goebl W., et al., *The Piano Action as the Performance Interface*, Proceedings of the Stockholm Acoustics Conference, 2003

Goebl W. et al., *Once Again, The Perception of piano touch and tone*, Proceedings of the International Association on Musical Acoustics, 2004, Nara, Japan

Gombrich, E.H., *In Search of Cultural History* Clarendon Press

Gombrich, E. H., *New York Review of Books*, March 4, 1993

Hoffman, D. D., *Visual Intelligence*, W.W. Norton & Company; 2000

Hurpeau, Laurent (coord.) *Marie Jaëll*, a collective work. Symétrie Music Publishing, Lyon.

Jacob F., "Qu'est ce que la vie?" In *Université des Savoirs* (ed) Michaud Y, Odile Jacob, Paris 2000.

Jones, Howard Mumford, *Howard Mumford Jones: An Autobiography*. Harvard University Press, 1974

Katz, D. (1884-1953), *The World of Touch* (ed Lester E. Kruger), Lawrence Erlbaum Associates 1989

Koenigberger D., *Renaissance Man and Creative Thinking*, The Harvester Press, 1979

MacNeill, D. *Hand and Mind, What Gestures Reveal about Thought*, University of Chicago Press 1992

Monelle, R. "Music and Language" in *The Encyclopedia of Language and Linguistics*. Asher R.E. (ed.) Pergamon Press, Oxford 1994.

Pozzi, Catherine, *Journal*, Edition Ramsay, 1987

Rosen C., "On Playing the Piano," *The New York Review of Books*, October 21, 1999

Rosen C., and Zerner H., The Romantic Revolution, *The New York Review of Books*, Nov. 22, 1979

Rosen C., "The Chopin Touch," *The New York Review of Books* 1987, 9-13.

Rosen C., "Should We Adore Adorno," *The New York Review of Books*, October 24, 2002

Rosen C., "What did the Romantics Mean?" *The New York Review of Books*, Nov. 1, 1973

Rowland, D. (ed.), *The Cambridge Companion to the Piano*, Cambridge University Press, 1998

Saint-Saëns, Camille, *Portraits et Souvenirs*, Calman-Lévy

Schenker, H., *Harmony*, edited and annotated by O. Jones, translated by E. Mann Borgese, MIT Press, 1973

Searle, J.R, *The Mystery of Consciousness*, Granta Books, London 1997

Seeger, A.., "Music and Dance," *Companion Encyclopedia of Anthropology*, (ed.) T. Ingold, Routledge 1994 : 689

Sutherland D., "Domenico Scarletti and the Florentine Piano," *Early Music*, May 1995, 243-256

Weinreich, G. "The Coupled Motion of Piano Strings," *ibidem*

Zeki, S. "Art and the Brain," in *The Brain*, (ed.) Edelman G.M. and J.-P. Changeux

INDEX